<u>This is Me</u>

By Steve Harding

ISBN 978-0-9567191-02

CONTENTS

[Dedication]

Even though I wrote this book mainly for my children and grand children, so they can have more than just memories of their dad and granddad, it's also for all my family and relatives and for a lot of close friends. You know who you are, because without the interaction of all of these people I wouldn't think the way I do. For instance, my trips to Australia and Canada and just being round my cousins at different stages of life opens your eyes, believe me when I say the grass is never greener, life is life just the scenery changes.

I also want to make people aware that everything in this book was written before my 40th birthday. So any views I had were up to that point in my life, just to see if my views change in latter life.

Thanks mum and dad, you didn't do a bad job on me; I do love you both very much, even though you have worn your trousers inside out and back to front at times mum. God bless you all…

Love Steve xxx.

[Introduction]

Who is he! I hear you say. Well, by the end of this book you should know me quite a bit better than you do now.

Inside you will find that rather than bore you with a life story of someone you don't know that goes on and on, I have just outlined my life up to the present time, then wrote things of significance that I remember or have done that will stay with me forever. There is a lot of stuff I have left out, which would of made the book drag on a bit, so with this in mind it's to the point and written the way I speak with no airs or graces. Also I have put in my diary, a personal fitness diary that I have kept that stretches more than ten years. This does go on a little bit I'm sad to say but it felt important to me that I put in every single date, that way if ever someone wanted to follow it they could. Good luck! . Also in the book is my philosophy's the way I see things, not necessarily the right way but right for me.

Why? Because when I was a kid my granddad John Underwood, used to tell me stories about his life and what he did, and as he got older and me and my brother's got bigger he was always comparing us to when he was a young man and how strong he was. He'd done his bit in the war then when he came out he used to be a ground worker and had his own gang of men that used to work for him. He was known for his strength and digging holes quicker than a JCB. But as he got really old I used to feel very sad for him, all he had was what was inside his head no proof of what he was like and nothing to compare him in his prime to me or my brothers in our prime.

When is your prime? Well it's a different time for everyone, that's why I kept a diary of all the different exercises I have done through different ages of my life, so that one day I can be honestly compared to my children and grandchildren or whoever and they can read what their dad or granddad was like, what I achieved and what I didn't achieve and how I thought and what made me laugh or cry.

My granddad passed away some time ago now, but he will live on in the few people he inspired, and thanks to him and my dad Roy Harding who have inspired me in their different ways, I can now help my children and one day my grandchildren to know me better.

I am a normal man with his story to tell I'm not famous, I'm Steve Harding and this is my story. I hope you like it, **cause this is me.**

CHAPTER 1

In the beginning...

Mum and dad where both born during the Second World War in 1942. Mum came

from a family of 9, The Underwood's she had five sisters and one brother and they all

lived in Windsor. Dad came from a family of 4 The Harding's with one brother, and

all originally came from London. My dad's family moved out of London after the

war, they were going to demolish a lot of the old houses in London to make way for

new roads and the rebuilding of London and it just so happened that the whole street

that dad lived on was ear-marked for demolition, so they were offered either to move

to White City in London or totally start a fresh in a new housing project in a place

called Britwell, which is what they decided to do, which was handy for me or I

wouldn't be here.

Britwell is very close to Slough trading estate which still is a very big industrial

estate with some very big and well known company's. It was at one of these

companies's where me mum and dad both met, at the age of 18. They were courting,

for three years and got married at 21. They called it courting then, we call it going out

with each other, I think courting sounds better though.

Not long after they were married me mum now Rosemarie Harding still 21 had a brain

haemorrhage. She was put on a bed of ice to try and stop the bleeding in her head, and was in

a coma for 3 months, my dad Roy Harding, was told by the doctor's she may need to have a

blood transfusion, but as mum and most of mum's family where Jehovah's witnesses the

family said no. But me dad being dad and not a Jehovah's witness said, "I'm next of kin I'm her husband, if she needs blood she'll have it", got the last word. Anyway after all the hassle mum didn't have to have blood and she came out of her coma and everyone was happy she'd survived. Mum and dad where told by the hospital they may never be able to have children as the pressure of labour may be to much for her head and could burst the blood vessel and she may die in labour. But they were wrong!

It all started about 5 years later, on June 19th 1970, I was born Stephen Grant Harding 8lb1oz a baby boy. Born at the Canadian Red Cross Hospital in Taplow, a minor miracle really, due to mum's former condition.

We all lived in a 3-bedroom house off of Burlington road in Burnham, near Slough. Mum and dad really adored me, being the first child and spent a lot of time making me happy. They took me to Canada with them when I was just 15 months old to see one of mum's sister's, Joy who also had recovered from a brain haemorrhage.

Not that I remember any of the trip, but mum and dad told me I was a bit hyperactive then and they couldn't take their eyes off me for a minute. Actually if you asked my family they would probably say I'm still hyper now.

As a child I had one of those big old Silver Cross navy blue prams with the big wheels and the suspension frames; you know, the one that looks like a royal carriage. One day mum put me in the garden asleep in me royal carriage and the next time she checked on me I was hanging on the outside of it in mid air feet kicking with me cardigan caught on one of the hood clasps. I was very active and would keep them on their toes, but not the only problem as mum was expecting another little miracle. Brother Wayne in 1972.

Mum had her hands full, dad working as a tool setter on Slough industrial estate during the day and mum looking after Wayne and me during the day, then working part time in the evenings. In the summer I can remember being out all day and getting up to all sorts, don't get me wrong I wasn't that bad and generally I was a good kid but I had me moments like all kids do.

I won't tell you to much read the news paper article that I have copied into this book but what I will say is there was a fire, my friend David was under a bed and he set light to the

2

covers, it was layers of covers on a bed in those days no duvet and instead of lighting the fire on the covers wall side so he could get out, he lit them on the overhang on the outside of the bed, while he was still underneath, so when it went up in flames he was stuck under there.

He was panicking a bit, as the flames were quite big and there was a lot of smoke. I was shouting to him to get out but he was scared and wouldn't get out so I put my arm under the flames and just dragged him out by the first thing I got hold of which was his hair, we then made a hasty retreat out of the house. It got me name in the papers as you can see by the picture of me at three. I didn't feel like much of a hero though after being told off for playing with matches. So it wasn't long before I was shipped off to nursery to give mum a break and to keep me occupied. It didn't keep me occupied for long, I can vaguely remember Santa Clause coming to see all the kids at Christmas and me ripping his beard off saying "that's not Santa Claus that's so en so's dad". So when I was four, they sent me to big school, well Lent Rise Junior and Infant school in Burnham to be precise.

I bloody hated my new school, mum would drop me off and the teachers would have to hold me back crying till mum went out of sight. But after a while I'd cotton on and be as good as gold for the teachers, say bye to mum she'd give me a kiss and that was that, no teachers holding me back or nothing, lovely I thought. When mum was outside the school gates I'd run round to the other gate go out over the main road and hide in someone's garden and wait for mum to come past then slowly follow her back home ducking in and out of peoples garden's so she couldn't see me, I would then keep an eye on the house and wait for mum to go out to the shop's or go to a friend's house, then I'd go home get through a window and hide under the bed or in a cupboard or something, it was my little surveillance operation at 4 or 5 years old. They got me to stay at school in the end, but I was seriously not happy. I thought if mum and dad loved me so much how could they leave me here and why can't I just go back home with her.

I was still having a bottle at five years old and I used to have it filled with milk with about two-tea spoon's full of sugar in it, which probably contributed to my hyperactivity. So when I did eventually throw my bottle in the bin, I was bored.

3

I had to be doing something all the time so I don't know if it was a boredom thing or I just wanted some more attention off of mum and dad, but for some strange reason every time I was bored I started pulling on my hair, not great clumps but strand by strand, ok it doesn't sound that bad, but when its about 30 or 40 strands a night it doesn't take long before you start going bald.

When mum and dad caught me pulling it they would shout over to me, "Stephen! Stop pulling your hair". When I think back it makes me laugh but at the time it wasn't funny. I don't know why, I couldn't stop doing it; I was pulling it out by the bloody roots.

By this time there were 3 of us boy's mum had me brother Darren in 1975. So now there were 3 boys and one was going bald at 6 years old. So they decided to take me to the doctor's. Our doctor was about 4 miles away in Britwell so it was nearly an 8 mile round trip and as mum or dad couldn't drive it was a bloody long walk for little me in between dad giving me piggyback's. Dad's excuse for not driving was that he spent the money he had saved for a car on his wedding to me mum. Anyway you could cut a lot of time off of the walk to the doctor's if you went through this path way called piggy path, which was a long path through woods which used to crap the shit out of me, but I always felt safe with dad as he used to be a bit of a boxer in his time and he'd had his fair share of hassle growing up in London. When we saw the doctor he gave me this medicine that was supposed to make me stop pulling my hair, Gould knows how medicine is going to stop me arms moving to me head, but I took it anyway. After a few days of taking the medicine I started to eat a lot more than normal and it was doing nothing for me bald problem, I was still pulling it out like a good'un, so it was back to the doctors a couple of days later. This time the doctor said "Tie mittens to his hands and he won't be able to get to the strands of hair". The next day I've bitten holes in the end of the mittens and me fingers are poking out of the end doing their job on me head again, it was like they had a life of their own.

So there was now us three boys under seven and one had a bald spot on his head for three helicopters to land on let alone one, who used to skip school at every opportunity and was a bit hyper.

Wayne at nursery school and Darren a baby with all his needs. It was no wonder that mum was at her Witt's end, every once in a while mum would stay at one of her sisters for a couple of day's for a break.

After a few years' things got a little easier for mum, we were all at school and mum used to be at home hoping that the phone didn't go and there was a problem with one of us at school.

But the days may have been easier for mum but they were a lot harder for me. As I was getting older and the kid's were getting wiser with age, as they do, they began to realise that having a big bald spot in the middle of your head at 7,8 and 9 years of age wasn't a normal thing and I used to be called loads of names and had no friends at school, except for Martin who was my next door neighbour and even he was put into another class, because he was a few months younger than me and fell into the year below. Don't get me wrong I wasn't physically bullied, I could take care of myself, and did on many occasions it was just the loneliness of not having anyone to play with at school, that hurt. The only time the kid's would speak to me was at break time when they were playing chase and no one could catch a certain kid because he was to fast, as I was a good runner they would include me in the game until I caught him then I would be out again. Those few years of my life were the worst and have made me partly who I am today and gave me the drive and will to try to be something and to do my best at everything I do. As you would find out if you spoke to my family and close friends.

I always had my little bag packed under my bed ready to run away, but if I hadn't of had such a good dad who was always taking us boy's out and the thought of crisps and coke every Thursday night while watching Steve Austin the "six million dollar man", when dad got paid, maybe I would have gone, who knows. It is the little things when you are a kid that keep you going. I remember walking to Burnham High Street every Sunday morning with dad to get the papers and a packet of Opal Fruits (Star Bursts now) if I was lucky.

Dad was very fair with all of us, if we played up and dad was getting mad I used to have the shivers cause if he hit you round the legs you bloody felt it, but we were well loved by them both and we loved them and gave them the respect they deserved.

5

It's at this point that I would like to say that there's a difference between smacking your kids on the legs or bum and beating them black and blue and causing them harm.

At no point in our growing up did a whack round the legs for misbehaving do any of us any harm.

Between 1979/80 mum and dad decided to move. They applied for and got a brand new 3-bed room house in Lent Green Lane, still in Burnham, a brand new estate they had just finished building. It was about a mile away from our old house and the Smith's, they were our neighbours and where my one and only friend Martin lived. We went back a long way with the Smith's us boy's, we used to climb the fence and go into their garden and they used to do the same and climb into ours. We had a plumb tree in our garden and in the summer holidays we used to all climb the tree and sit up there and eat the plumbs. They were a family of 5, Steve and Carol mum and dad and Samantha Martin and Danny were the kids, we all had some very good times together, including the street party for the 1977 silver jubilee which took place on our local green, what a glorious sunny day that was.

We now lived further away from Martin and Danny and had a longer walk to school, so mum would get me and Wayne up dressed washed and had breakfast and out the door by 7.45am, we would get to Martin and Danny's by 8am and they would never be ready so Carol would do me and Wayne another breakfast while we were waiting for Martin and Danny. Then on the way to school if we were lucky enough to catch the milkman on the end of his round we sometimes jumped on the back of the milk float and hitched a ride to school.

But this wasn't going to last, mum gave birth to our sister Nicola, which put pay to the football team I thought mum was going to have, this meant another move as we now needed a 4 bed room house. So after only being in that house 10 months mum and dad decided, well mum decided really, that we were going to move out of the area and move to Bracknell to be closer to mum's parent's, brother and sisters. Mum had 5 sisters and 1 brother but one of her sisters lived in Canada and another lived in Australia, but the rest lived in Bracknell and Windsor. Nice for mum to be closer to her family but this was going to be a big step for dad as he worked on Slough Industrial Estate as a tool setter setting power presses and as he

6

couldn't drive it was almost impossible for him to get to work, there was no direct buses to Slough industrial estate from Bracknell, so dad was going to have to stay at his mum and dad's who lived in Britwell. Dad would stay there during the week and come home weekends. Bracknell was an up and coming town with big computer firms, nothing for a tool setter here. That was their problem, mine was Martin and Danny, would I ever see them again, me Wayne and Darren were going to miss our Friends. There were a hundred reasons why we shouldn't move and only one as far as I was concerned why we should. I was going to change school. *Yippee!*

CHAPTER 2

A new decade…

The year was 1981 we ended up living in Bracknell in a three-bed room house in a place called Harmans Water. Even though the house was to small mum said it would be a stepping-stone and that once we were in Bracknell we could then apply for a four-bed room house.

After about three months of moving to Bracknell dad was made redundant from his job in Slough. Bad for mum and dad but good for us kids, as we would now see dad during the week as well as weekends. Dad always had time for us kids so we loved him being home.

Me and Wayne were doing alright at school, you know how it is new kids new school, we got into a few fights as you do but I was treated normal, I don't know who the kids used to be horrible to but it wasn't me and I was thankful for that. But the kid's used to go up to my brother Wayne and ask him what happened to my head, why was I bald in the middle. Wayne used to get so sick of it he used to make up things and say "a bit of wet plaster fell off the ceiling and landed on his head and when he tried to pull it off it pulled his hair off". Cheer's Wayne! Oh yes and there was one that it was a birthmark.

By now I was getting very conscious of myself, it didn't matter when I was young I didn't care how I looked, but now I was nearing a teenager how would I get a girl friend like this, I thought to myself. It wasn't until I was 12 years old that I found out

I had a bit of a lisp to. I wasn't aware of it until a friend started talking funny to me and when I asked him why he spoke certain words funny he said that he was copying me and that was how I spoke. So in the space of a few months I corrected the way I spoke and pulled my hair less and finally stopped at about 13. But it was to late, as after about 7 years non-stop of pulling it out by the roots there were parts that were never going to grow again and even now as an adult I still have parts that don't grow. The urge to start pulling it again never goes either, it's always there but then again millions of other men have gone completely bald so it just looks as if it's natural now but we know different don't we.

It has only been recently that I found the correct name for the condition, which is *Trichotillomania*. I know there are more sufferers out there who do the same thing and now looking back I know the cure is to get him or her a doll or something with hair, that they can have in their hands to keep their fingers busy, so they pull the hair out of the doll instead of themselves.

We all moved a couple of more times still in Bracknell though, once to Crown Wood and then finally to a new house in Forest Park where we finally settled. It was a nice big house with woodland all around, for us kids it was great we used to build camps in the woods and to have all that space was excellent.

Wayne and me were at our senior school called *Brakenhale,* Darren was at junior school and Nicola was at home.

It was always tight for money in our house; dad was now gardening part-time, and not being able to get full time work in the recession of the 80's, he had to do something. Mum was doing either early morning or evening cleaning part time, and it was very hard for them to keep us all satisfied Things were a lot dearer now me and Wayne were older, we were into BMX bikes, skateboards and roller skates and there was no way they could buy two or three of these sort of toys, so poor old Darren used to get the hand-me-downs, mum and dad used to do us proud though, but if we wanted stuff we had to get it ourselves. Wayne used to help the milkman in the mornings and I had an early morning paper round, we also started caddying for golfers at the *Berkshire golf course* which was situated a short bike ride through the woods at the back of our house, it was good money for kids of our age and you saw some famous faces to,

we used to get about £6 pound a round or about £15 for the day. After a while we would go further a field to *Wentworth* and *Sunningdale* golf courses, not bad for 11 and 13 year olds.

Mum's sister our aunt Joy asked if we would all like to go and visit her and our uncle Ted in Canada for a couple of weeks. But there was no way mum and dad could afford all of us to go so only me Wayne and mum would go as Darren and Nicola were to young to really remember it, but Wayne and me had to save our own spending money, which we did through caddying.

We had never been on a plane before, well I had but I was only a baby, we were going to remember this journey and were very excited. All our friends thought dad had a pools win or something.

But we had all worked hard as a family for months for this trip; it was just unfortunate that dad and the others couldn't come.

We saw our aunt and uncle for the first time and stayed on the farm that they managed, it had a lovely big white wooden house, it had a pond that we used to fish in and a swing that was tied to an old tree in the front garden that my uncle had put up for his children, my cousins that had now grown up and left home. It was exactly how you would picture a farm in Canada, but with one special thing, our auntie and uncle lived on this one and we loved it. They took us to see Niagara Falls and took us to loads of great places, so when it was time for coming home you can bet Wayne and me were upset. I think I cried for about a week when I got home, dad felt a bit bad that I was that upset, he started to think that he wasn't providing for us very well and we should all be more happier than we were. But it wasn't that at all, I was so upset because it had taken us such a lot of time and effort to get to Canada that I was scared that we might never see our auntie and uncle again. But two years later dad Wayne and Darren went, and little did I know then, but that trip to Canada that I went on was just the beginning of my many travels as an adult.

We made some good friends in Bracknell and I will always remember cycling all the way to Ascot to see my auntie Val and my cousins, then onto see my uncle Ray who lived a bit further on.

We always wondered about the Smiths though, Martin and Danny. So one-day mum said give them a call and invite them over. So we did. And every six months or so they used to come and stay for a week and they were the best weeks of our lives when we all got back together. We had to say to our other friends that they were our cousins, other wise they would get the hump that we would not play with them for that week, and to try and explain everything about our past friendship with Martin and Danny to them was just not worth it.

As time went on and we were all teenagers I started to wonder what I wanted to do with my life. Watching mum and dad struggle through the years made me want to do something with my life and earn some big money so we could all live a little better, so I thought I would become an actor. So this was my mission, I chose drama as one of my options at school and also started at stage school at 14 years old. I also went on later to do a production of Charlie girl at the wild theatre in Bracknell, for another production company. I also attended a theatre lighting workshop at the same theatre and went for auditions and got a part in the production of Alice in wonderland. For a while it was all going ok, but then things started to change. I was unable to attend auditions because they were to far away and neither mum nor dad could drive, also the school careers officer said that when all actors start off they struggle at first and may need to have a job to keep the money coming in. So I put the acting on hold and got a job. When I left school in the recession of the eighty's the local council were running the Youth Training Scheme Y.T.S., where you train in a particular job for two years on crap money and get a trade behind you. Well my trade was painting and I enjoyed it. We'd go out in gangs of about six and paint all different places like houses, schools and churches it was great, we also went on a works trip to the New Forest, which I have wrote a bit more about in one of my little true stories further on in the book.

We were all getting quite good at the painting lark, so after about a year or so the council decided to send all of us to college in Reading for one day a week for our City and Guilds certificates.

There must have been about 10 of us at the time going to college one day a week all working on different placements with different decorating firms and meeting up to attend college once a week.

I was working on a building site with some real good decorating firm painting houses from bare wood right up to completion; we even painted the show house. So when the college teachers tried to show us how to paint on bits of board they bit off more than they could chew, they treated us like kids painting on bits of scrap wood. For shit sake I was painting £300,000 pound houses four days of the week now I'm painting on a bit of board. We told the teacher of our displeasure and he said that

"You will be treated the same as every other class". I asked the teacher if they taught us to paint radiators on this course and he said, "No why should we." Oh great I thought after three years of doing this course and getting our City and Guilds certificates if someone asked us to paint a radiator we wouldn't know were to start. Luckily for me I was painting radiators on site. But we were all bored with the course, being treated like we knew nothing, alright we had only been painting for just over a year but the work we were doing was just about everything you could think of and had to be a very high standard.

To cut a long story short we all ended up getting chucked off the course. I left the decorating firm I was with because I left the Y.T.S. and started with a new firm on proper money.

By the way I'm not telling you the names of some of the company's or firms I have worked for cause some of them are still going now. Not that I have anything bad to say about *most* of them but I don't know if they would like me to mention them, so I won't.

I had just passed my driving test on the 1st of September 88. I was eighteen, the first in the family to drive that included mum and dad and their parents, but I hadn't saved up enough money for a car cause I'd spent most of it on the bloody lessons, so I needed a few months graft to get some cash behind me. I was earning some good money working for this guy doing home improvements, we would normally work together but on occasion he would leave me at a job while he went to another. After a while he said to me that if he didn't have to pick me up in the mornings and I could make my own way to the jobs he would up my money. I knew I wouldn't be able to get a car for a while so I thought I'd buy a moped to get me about from job to job until I could get a car, so that's what I did, I bought a little Tomos 50cc moped out of me mum's catalogue, I could easily afford the monthly payments and was saving at the same time. Mean while me old mate Martin was also working, as a printer in a small firm in Maidenhead and his dad used to like motorbikes, so Martin had passed his motorbike test and was well on his way up the bikes, getting onto the bigger machines. He used to come over every once in a while and on occasion take me on the back for a spin each time on a bigger bike. So when I phoned him up and said I'd just bought a Tomos moped, I had to take the phone away from my ears cause his laughter was deafening, and went even louder when I told him I'd got it from me mum's catalogue. "When you said you were thinking about getting a motorbike I thought you would be getting a big one not a hair dryer". He said. Well I wasn't into bikes like him, the only bikes I was into were pushbikes, I was more interested in getting a car. But to this day he reminds me of my moped, I used to call it my GPZ900 Tomos, 30mph on the straight and 32 down hills, what G force.

I had the moped for less than a month when tragedy struck in the shape of a car. Yes a car on a roundabout hit me. I had a red moped a white crash helmet a yellow ski jacket and blue tracksuit bottoms on and the woman driver said she didn't see me; maybe I didn't stand out enough eh. Anyway I could see the car come onto the roundabout just as I was going to turn off, it was coming straight at me and as my GPZ900 Tomos wasn't that quick I couldn't avoid her, all I could do was lift my left leg up so it wouldn't get hit but unfortunately the car drove over the moped a bit and broke my right leg underneath it. I couldn't and didn't want to believe that I had a broken leg so I tried to stand up, which just pushed the bones on top of each other so it looked like I had a golf ball under my skin. I loved sports and was always running and the thought that my running days were over was just too much.

I spent two weeks in the hospital and eight months in plaster, and a whole year off work because I had a few complications. I will always remember going over the Forest Park Social Club with me dad on some evenings to have a pint or two and having to balance myself home on me crutches.

When I did eventually get out of plaster I couldn't recognise my right leg, all the muscle had deteriorated due to lack of use and the left one wasn't much better either, as although I didn't injure it I still couldn't run or do my normal things so it to was a little worse for wear, It took months before I was able to start running on it properly again.

When I look back on it all now I feel such a fool. I think that half the reason that it didn't heal quicker, is that I was so negative about it, as being in plaster for so long I began to think I would never get out of it and lost all confidence that it was going to heal. I say to you now that if an unfortunate event happens and you do end up in plaster or you are ill have confidence and look on the positive and not the negative or you will make things worse, I have learnt the hard way.

At this point, I would just like to thank mum and dad and family and friends for all the support especially to mum and dad through that year, I know it was tough for you both, as well as me.

I got several thousand pound insurance pay out for that accident, and after the year or so I had just been through I decided I would see a bit more of the world. So I asked Martin if he would like to come to Australia with me, we both had relations out there I had mum's sister my auntie Eileen and my uncle Ian and all of my cousins and Martin had his dad's brother his uncle Brian and his auntie Brenda and all his cousins out there also. So we had plenty of people to see and places to go. Martin said he would love to go. Ok now there's a difference between saying and doing, Martin had a lot more to lose than I did; he had a steady job a new motorbike and was sorting himself out. I had another job working in a warehouse just to tide me over until the day of our departure and that was it. Martin said he would sell his motorbike to get money for the trip; I was going to buy his ticket he just had to get his spending money. He loved his bikes and I knew the day he sold his bike he was coming.

Every man and his dog said they would come with us, I think they thought we weren't serious, but we knew that when it was time to get the tickets they wouldn't go. I wouldn't go half way round the world with someone I didn't trust, but me and Martin had years of friendship behind us and we knew that if either of us got into any situation we could rely on the other one 100%. On the 18th of June 1990 one day before my 20th birthday we took off, Australia here we come.

CHAPTER 3

On my travels…

I hadn't been on a plane for quite a while; the last time, was when I went to Canada as a teenager with mum and Wayne in 83", and I don't think Martin had been on a jumbo jet until that moment, so we were looking forward to our extra long trip to Australia on a Singapore airlines 747. This was going to be a trip to remember and we were both looking forward to it and going to try and do our best to enjoy it.

We couldn't believe our eyes when we got a look at the stewardesses on the plane, they were all beautiful oriental women, you could have chucked me any one of them and I would have been happy, every time I looked at Martin, his eyes were fixed on their bum's and his mouth was open. I hope he wasn't going to stay like that for the full 12 hours, which was how long it was going to take us just to get to Singapore. The flight was good, and Singapore airlines cabin crew were great.

On arriving at Singapore we were greeted by this beautiful airport fully air-conditioned with waterfalls and everything, it had been voted best airport for about 5 years running and it deserved it. We had a 10 hour wait at the airport until our connecting flight was due for Australia, so we thought we would go outside and have a look round, but we were wrong, they wouldn't let us out of the airport as we weren't visiting Singapore and did not have the entry visa's to get in. Now this was a nice airport but to spend 10 hours in it was going to make it a not so nice airport. We found a way to get out of the airport on one of their excursions of the city, but on condition we handed over our passports to the lady organiser before we step foot outside the airport, then on return they would give our passports back. I didn't like the idea of handing over my passport, but it was the only way we were going to get out of the airport and into that glorious sun, so we did.

As soon as the door opened to the outside and we left the air-conditioning behind, it hit us 98 degrees farenheight and 99% humidity. I had on a pair of jeans and a denim jacket I had sweat on me brow just walking over the road to the coach it was like being in a sauna, On entering the coach and finding my seat I reached for the air-conditioning above my head, which wasn't much cop seeing as a part of it had just come off in my hand, at the same time the lady with the passports was saying "Be gentle with the air con in the coach as any damages will have to be paid for". What a lovely trip that was in between attractions I was trying to stuff this bit of plastic back into the hole it had came out of. What we did see of Singapore was lovely and we swore we were going to definitely come back and visit their longer next time.

We were now back at the airport, back on the next leg of the trip, the 5-hour flight to Perth Australia, at which point it had suddenly dawned on me that I was going to see relatives I had never seen before, I hope they were going to like me I thought. I had seen my auntie Eileen and my cousin Andrew before when they came over to England when I was young but my uncle Ian and my other three cousins I had never met, mum had always told me about them and I had seen photographs of them all as kid's but they were all men now all older than me cause this was mum's oldest sister and she had started her family years before I was around.

My auntie Eileen, Andrew and Kayleen his wife met us at Perth airport very early in the morning, and we stayed with Andrew and his family for a few days in their home opposite a very picturesque estuary in a place called Mandura. I will never forget seeing that lemon tree in their back garden, there not the kind of thing you see in

England. That wasn't our final destination though; we were aiming for the mining town of Wickam, with a few stops in between.

Wickam was where my auntie Eileen my uncle Ian and my other two cousins lived. Situated about a 700 miles up the west coast of Australia.

After a few days with Andrew and his family we set off on the greyhound bus service to the next port of call, my cousin Jim's at Dongara, which is on the way to Wickam.

Now these buses aren't like the green line back home, you can't just stick out your hand and get on, you have-to buy your ticket in advance and it may only stop at that stop once a day or once a week at a set time and your time could be 3 in the morning or 3 in the afternoon, so if you miss it you have got a bloody long wait for the next one. These coaches are built like tanks, with these bloody great roo-bars on the front of them and wire meshing over the window-screen so if they do hit anything the bus hasn't got to stop. You never know what you could hit at night in the desert, kangaroos, snakes, camels or flocks of birds.

When we arrived at Jim's in Dongara, Marty and I gave him a hug and he took us on the short drive back to his house. When we got there Martin immediately saw Jim's motorbike and started looking round it, I could tell it was making him think of his own bike, but he had no regrets as we were half way round the world now in Australia, he could buy a motorbike any time. We had only been there 10 minutes and Jim asked Martin if he would like a go on his bike, the next thing I see is Martin on the bike with Jim's crash helmet on and Jim explaining where he should ride it and what road's he should take to get back to the house. After about 10 minutes there was no sign of Marty, that's what the aussies called him; all we could hear was the noise of the motorbike in the distance, one minute we would hear him close and see him flash by at the top of the road, next minute we would see him in the distance on a different road going the opposite way. He was lost; I was running to the top of the road hoping he would come by so I could wave him in the right direction, but every time I would get to the top of one road he would be at the end of another, it was like something out of a carry on film. All I could think about was what would happen if the cop's got hold of him. How would he explain; he was on a motorbike that wasn't his, he didn't know where he was going and had no Australian licence. In the end I was laughing so much I had to sit on the grass and just wait until he finally took the right road the house was on.

Over the next few days with Jim and his kid's he would take us fishing and take us out in his car, which he called the beast, because of the size of it and he would tell us story's about what life was like in Wickam and what my other two cousins John and Nigel were like. By now we had heard quite a bit about Wickam some good and some bad and were wondering if we were going to like it right up there in the middle of nowhere.

Jim and his Family waved us off on the greyhound coach on a sunny afternoon and what lied ahead was a trip through the night and most of the next day. Apart from the roadhouses where you stop for food and to pick up people our next stop would be Wickam.

It was about 6.20am I looked out of the coach window and all I could see was this beautiful sun making its way up into the clear blue sky and the start of another day, I looked over to Marty to see if he was awake and could see him just opening his eyes and at the same time sort of squinting as the sun hit his face. "We will be approaching wickam in about five minutes" the driver said. We started getting our things together and I was getting ready to see my uncle Ian for the first time, I looked out of the coach window and saw a sign coming up and it read welcome to Wickam but underneath someone had sprayed on; keep Wickam clean wash a pome; Oh bloody lovely I thought. We had heard the stories that us English keep coal in the bath and don't wash for weeks on end.

It had taken us a week to get to Wickam from England with the stop over and we were going to stay in Wickam for a while now that we had finally got there. My uncle Ian was waiting for us at the bus stop and put our gear in the back of the car and drove us for about two minutes to their house. Now to the people who lived in Wickam and worked for the mining company, it probably seemed like just another boring mining town but to me and Martin it was great, my uncle Ian worked as a butcher in the next town and during the day we could use his old Volvo car to drive to all the different beaches in the area, I mean it was July so it was winter in Australia but it was still in the 70's in Wickam cause it was so far up the west coast. Every beach we went to was empty cause the locals thought it was to cold to go into the water, but that didn't stop Marty or me, we would be swimming, snorkelling and sun bathing during the day, while my cousins were at work and going to the club to play pool with my cousins in the evenings. Just being with them made it good for me and they got on well with Marty to.

I remember once we were snorkelling at Settlers Beach and we saw this big black shadow go past under the water in front of us, I immediately thought of Jaws the movie and big white teeth, so to say I got out of the water bloody quick would be an understatement, and I could hear by the splashing of the water behind me that Marty wasn't far behind, I then looked round to see Marty had stopped running and was just looking at the water. "It's ok" he shouted, "It's a dolphin", "they still have teeth don't they" I replied. " Yes but they won't attack humans" he shouted. Now I have known

Marty a bloody long time and during that time on no occasion has Marty been to university to become the leading authority on marine behaviour, but I must admit it was a lovely sight to see, dolphins swimming about in front of you. We still laugh at the thought of us two seeing the shadow of the dolphin in front of us and exiting the water at top speed.

In the evening we would go to the only club or pub the town had with John or Nigel and occasionally we would go to Point Samson where they had a fish and chip shop near the beach that sold real fresh fish and they sold so many kinds half we had never heard of, it was great. It was going to take a lot to beat this place when we moved on.

I had been to the police station and showed them my British driving licence and eventually got an Australian one. I did this for two reasons one was so I could use it for ID to open a bank account, because it had your photo on it and you don't travel with your money on you all the time and two if I was to be done for any traffic violations they would take the Australian licence and not my British one. While I had been going through all this me and Marty couldn't help wondering who took people for their driving tests in this town cause there's no driving schools, probably half the people didn't even have a licence and after chatting to the cop's for a while they said that they do the tests and take people out. My cousin John said he would give Marty a few lessons in his car if he wanted to go for his test. So Marty booked a test date up with the cop's for two week's later. Marty was a bit apprehensive about the test being in two week's but he was going to go for it anyway, so the lessons began.

Marty was having his lessons in my cousin's 4.1Litre Ford Falcon and had about 5 lessons in the two week's and then the day had come for the test. We got in the cop shop a little early and waited inside and then he was gone out the door with a cop and into john's car. He must have only been gone 10 minutes when in he walks back into the police station; I immediately thought that his driving was that bad the cops had to bring him back, because Marty has got poor vision, but when I asked him what was wrong he said nothing I've passed. The coppa had taken him round the block made him reverse in the police station car park and said to him he'd passed, Marty said he'd buy him a drink over the club that night and that was it, done and dusted.

Marty had a full Australian driving licence and I knew that when we got back to England he could transfer it for a full English licence. What a jammy sod, all the money I had spent on my lessons and test back home and his had cost him probably a tenner and a drink. What a place to take a test though no traffic lights, roundabouts, zebra crossings nothing but straight dusty roads with the occasional turn. Good luck to him, this meant we both were driving now and would enjoy the holiday even more.

The time had come to move on, we had been in wickam for just over two months and we wanted to see some more of Australia and eventually make our way over to Melbourne to see Marty's family. We went to the local travel shop to book our tickets on the greyhound, we had decided that we were going to take a week to get to Melbourne with stops at Ayres Rock and Alice Springs for a couple of days. And the good thing about going by coach is that you see everything, we still had to pick people up at other towns on the way so we would end up seeing all of the west coast of Australia and coming down from Darwin through the centre of Australia into the Northern Territory to Alice Springs.

We were going to miss Wickam, but most importantly for me I was going to miss my relatives and all the people we had met on our stay there we were treated so well by every one, thank you all for making me and Marty so welcome.

I knew it wasn't going to be the last I saw of Wickam and I would be back.
We went on to Alice Springs, where we stayed for one night in a back packers hostel,

I think it was about $5.00 dollars a night, or about £2.40 in English. The next morning we caught a coach to Ayres Rock, or; Ularu as the aborigines called it; Now Ayres Rock doesn't seem a lot from the bottom but believe me it is quite a climb. Our coach driver said that if anyone was going to climb the rock and they felt like they were going to have a heart attack on the way up, they should jump off, so that it looked like you had fallen, because everyone that had ever fallen had a plaque put up in remembrance. We needed him dint we. We did climb the rock and signed the book at the top and it was an amazing experience and the views were breathtaking.

We were staying at the complex that was dedicated especially for Ayres Rock and the Olgas, another mountain range that was in the middle of the desert. At the complex we met this English girl, I think her name was Karen, who also went to Ayres Rock with us and then travelled on with us to Dandenong near Frankston Melbourne, which is where Marty's relatives lived.

While we were there we were staying with Marty's Uncle Brian and Auntie Brenda, and we got to know all his cousins and their families quite well, they even let Karen stay in their home for a few days until she moved on.

We had done a fair bit of travelling around Melbourne. We had been to the zoo and down the river, and on a trip to New South Wales to go to the casino and we had a good time their for a couple of months but this wasn't like western Australia, it rained here a bloody lot the weather was much like England, so I decided to travel back to Wickam to western Australia and spend Christmas with my relatives and Marty had decided he would stay here with his. I thanked Brian and Brenda for having me and was off back on me old friend the greyhound bus on over a 2000-mile coach trip back to Wickam.

I was now on my own and things are a bit different travelling thousands of miles on your tod, you have-to be that much more aware I mean I was going to be sleeping on this coach for a couple of days with different people getting on and off the coach, even through the night, so you never really get a lot of sleep, but that is all part of the trip and I wasn't going to let it stop me from seeing this wonderful country.

I was going back to Wickam across the bottom of Australia past Adelaide through the Nulabore plane with a stop at the Great Australian Bite then onto Kalgooley over to Perth and back up the 700-miles up the west coast to Wickam.

I got Christmas out of the way, which was different having Christmas in the heat and decided to go back home in the middle of January. I phoned Marty to see how he was and to tell him my plans; he had decided to stay a bit longer and eventually came home in April, having stayed out there for 10 months in total. My total stay in Australia was 7 months and in that time I had travelled over nearly all of Australia and the experiences we had were unforgettable. The only part of Australia we hadn't seen was from Sydney up the east coast to Carnes, but if ever I were to go again that would be where I would go.

At eighteen I had a broken leg, was in plaster for eight months had a year of work and was at the lowest of lows and to have done all this in that short time, you never know what life has in store for you. Mind you, you have to help yourself to, I mean I didn't have to spend my accident money on the trip of a lifetime; I could have spent it on anything.

CHAPTER 4

*B*ack in the rat race...

I had phoned Wayne from Australia and confirmed my flight details with him and he

had told me he had just bought a new car, a B.M.W. and was going to pick me up

from Heathrow airport in it. Now when Wayne told me he had just bought a B.M.W. I

was thinking what sort of state will this car be in, I mean he was only 18 and the kind

of money you are looking at for a decent Beemer was quite a bit and that wasn't

including insurance, so I was expecting a right rust bucket and half expecting to be

doing a Flintstones when I got in it.

Wayne and me dad picked me up at Heathrow Airport at about 6.30 am on a cold

January morning it was good to see them after 7 months. We said our hellos in the

arrivals hall and then it was off to the car park. I was looking out for the worst

B.M.W. in the car park with different coloured wings no tread on the tyres and a coat

hanger for an aerial, but it was no where to be seen, instead we were heading for this

really nice one, I thought he's winding me up here, his car is on the opposite side he's

just going to pretend and walk to this nice one, at which point he pulls out his keys

opens the boot chucks me bag in and said "get in then". I couldn't believe this motor

was his, "how the hell did you get this?" I said to him. Apparently, he said that when I

left for Australia he got a bit inspired and wanted to do something with his life to, so

he had kept his head down really worked hard at the roofing, got a bit of money

behind him and was now wearing designer clothes and driving this B.M.W., mind you the insurance was dearer than the car as you would expect for an eighteen year old driving a 6 cylinder 2 litre 320 B.M.W.

Wayne is one of those blokes who get bored very quickly and it wasn't long before he was asking me if I wanted to buy his B.M.W off of him. Well I needed some wheels to get a job, so I bought it from him and also started paying the extortionate amount of insurance that went with it. Some young lads probably wouldn't have paid the insurance and drove illegally, but we had spent a lot of time getting the money for our driving lessons and getting things for our selves so we weren't going to risk losing our licences for no one.

I started work about 2 months later in a stationary warehouse, doing the late shift 1.30pm to 10.30 pm picking customer orders for next day delivery. I had a good eye for detail and liked things done properly so I fitted in with what they wanted quite quickly and I enjoyed the job and the money was good.

Over the next few months of 91 Martin had come home from Australia to and had got his old job back as a printer. It was amazing how quickly you got back into the old routine and before long we were back in the rat race as if we had never been away. Everything seemed pointless now, working all week just to go out on weekends or spend money on keeping the car on the road. I wanted more out of life than this, I was used to having goals to work for, I didn't mind working, we are all hard grafters in our family it was just I wasn't going to work and have nothing to show for it.

Martin's dad Steve was working at a stable in Burnham on weekends where he used to ride the horses and take the horses out for hacks. This had nothing to do with Steve's job, he just loved horses so enquired one day at a stable about riding and was able to ride out on the horses in exchange for doing bit's of work on the farm. His dad said to us come down the stables with me and learn to ride the horses then you can

27

come out with me on the hacks. At first we thought nar we won't bother the thought of sticking one of those skull caps on your head and having a crop in one hand and shouting "giddy up" didn't really appeal to us, but after a while I thought if ever we went back to Australia and we could ride we would be able go for a ride along the beach, cause they done quite a bit of that out there and it always seemed so lovely galloping along the beach just in the water.

So our no, eventually turned into a yer all right then we will come down the stables with you. So this was our goal every weekend for a few months we would go to the stables for a ride and every week we would get better and better until we were going out on hacks. We were getting quite familiar with every one down at the stables and used to get on ok with the stable girls to, in fact I remember those girls chasing me and Marty with a hand full of horse shite and throwing it at us and getting Marty on the back, I couldn't run for laughing, pay back I thought so I picked some shite up and chased after this girl and got her right in the face, what a shot. They also wanted to give us a running race around the field, cause one of these girls was a bit of a runner and they wanted to really rub our noses in it so to speak. Marty gave it a rain check, as he wasn't the best of runners but I said, " I'll give it a go". I'd been doing a bit of running to try and build my legs up after my accident so I was used to running a couple of miles or so, but they didn't know that. It was going to be 2 laps round the field, and just before we started more stable people came over to do the run, one of them told me that this girl who had challenged us to the run in the first place had never been beaten, lovely, nice to tell me on the start, oh well I was going to give it my best shot anyway. "Go" someone shouted and we were off, I started to think of Marty wiping the horse shite off of his top as I was running round the field and started laughing to myself. I was taking it easy over the first lap of the field, then this girl starts really going for it so of I go I'm up with her and we leave the rest of the stable people behind us. I am still behind her following her round the top half of the field, at one point I thought of running in front of her and putting some distance between us, but these girls didn't play anything fair and I thought if I had done that she would cut the corners of the field and run straight for the finish, so I just stayed with her so she thought I was tired and she was going to win and just hoped her finish wasn't to strong, then on the last forty metres or so I would take the lead and finish the race first, and fortunately that is what I did. When I finished Marty said, " well done mate, you should have heard them watching the race saying she's going to beat you that she had never lost a race, I knew you would win but I didn't tell them". We gave the girls a bit of stick and they gave as good as they got. It was a great laugh down there and we always had a good time, it's like when you were a kid and you think back to your summer holidays, it always seemed to be sunny and it was exactly the same there when I think back it was always sunny.

I was getting the 2-year itch as I used to call it. I wanted to get away again I could hear the call from the east coast of Australia calling this time. Sydney, Surfers Paradise, Cairns and the Great Barrier Reef, all the places we had missed the first time, I wanted to go back. I was going to ask Martin if he would go again, but to throw everything away for a second time was a lot to ask of him. He had got the second chance at his job and had a car and a motorbike he was really doing well, we had both lived a dream holiday once and to have that one bite of the apple is good enough but to do it again two and a half years later was a lot to achieve at our young ages, but would he do It? .

I said to Marty that I wouldn't blame him if he said no, I know you have a lot to lose but if I said I wanted to go back to Australia in June 93 to see the east coast would you come. He thought about it for a while and said yer I'm there. So that was it, all systems go. What you did was put a deposit on your tickets right away then pay them off weekly, that way you had something to work for and you don't have to come up with the money in one lump sum also you would lose your deposit if you cancelled so you didn't.

Thing's were going great I sold my sports car that I now had and bought an old banger and put the money away, we had a purpose, Danny, Martins brother who was two years younger had also made plans to go to Australia 4 months before us, he was going to see his relatives in Melbourne whom we had seen 2-years previous.

The plan was me and Marty were going to fly into Adelaide stay with my dad's cousin Ray and his family for two weeks, who I had never seen, then travel on the grey hound bus to Melbourne and pick Danny up from his relatives, the three of us would then travel up the east coast together. It all seems just a pipe dream when you are here in blighty, but that was our target and we were going for it.

We had the tickets paid off in the first year and all we had to do was save up some spending money. We weren't hermits and still used to go out every weekend but we just watched how much we spent. One weekend in July 92 we were invited to Martins auntie Janet's 40th birthday party Who lived in Wexham, Slough and although I got on ok with his auntie and his cousins I didn't really want to go to the party as I didn't know anyone else but them and Marty and I thought there would only be older people there, after all I was only 22 and Marty was 21. We did go in the end and that night changed my life forever.

On the night of the party, Janet his auntie said that we could stay for the night so that we could enjoy ourselves more and have a drink or several without having to drive home. We both agreed we would stay and tried to enjoy ourselves a bit more. As the night went on Marty's radar and mine had spotted two girls and they were both very nice, I said to Marty that I liked the dark haired one with big boobs that had her hair almost as short as mine. This was quite handy really as Marty liked the other girl she was talking to with the curly blonde hair. While we were chatting to Marty's cousin Andy and enquiring a bit more info about these two girls, as you do, the girls disappeared, shit! They have gone home we thought, "oh well it was good while it lasted. I'm going to get another drink do you want one," I said to Marty. "Yer all right mate" he said and I went into the kitchen to get another drink. While I was in there to my surprise the girl Marty liked came over to me and asked if I had noticed the other girl that she had been talking to, "what the dark haired one", I said, with the big tits I thought. "Yer", she said, " she quite likes you and wanted to know if you wanted to dance with her later". "Yer all right, what's her name", I said to her, "Karen" she said and walked back into the disco lit living room.

When it came to girls I was always a bit shy and still am, I would never make the first move, as far as I could tell if a girl asked me out I knew she liked me but if I asked them out I would never know if they really liked me or were just saying yes for a different reason. Marty on the other hand was the total opposite, he had the gift of the gab and wasn't afraid to use it, I remember him seeing four girls at once one time and all of them not knowing about the other.

I went back into the living room and couldn't wait to tell Marty my news, at which point I saw Karen the girl I was supposed to be dancing with later talking to Marty. I waited in the living room doorway until she had finished talking then went back over to Marty with his drink. "What did she want? Old bean" I said to him. "She wanted to know if I would dance with her mate Vicky later cause she really likes me", he said. "No! That Vicky bird came up to me and asked if I would dance with her mate Karen later as well".

Word must have got round that we were going to have dancing partners later that night, because everyone kept coming up to me telling me that Karen was single but she had a 9 year old son named Tony.

Nice of them to tell me but I didn't care I was going to Australia in the following June so wasn't looking for a relationship that was going to last. And I couldn't help but wonder how single Karen really was; I mean she was nearly five years older than me and attractive and where was Tony's dad. This was definitely going to be a one-night stand I thought to myself there were to many ifs and buts.

Eventually in the last hours of the night some slow songs came on, at witch point Marty and I didn't hesitate we went straight over to the girls and asked them to dance. Karen was 5ft 1in tall and I'm over 6ft so her head was in my chest while we were dancing, I wish it could have been the other way round but that's the way it was. We were both very shy me cause I always was and Karen because she knew most of the people at the party and she seemed to think they were all looking at her. I remember dancing with her to Lady in Red by Chris De Burgh and asking her if I could kiss her. Karen very shyly said yes but she felt a little uneasy and she went on to tell me that she had a 9-year-old son and that if I no longer wanted to dance with her she would understand and that she hadn't been in a relationship for a lot of years as she had been looking after Tony. "No one seems to want to know you if you have a child" she said. "I knew you had a son before I agreed to dance with you". I said to her. Tony Karen's boy was asleep on the sofa with semi drunk people sitting around him. Karen looked over to him and said that she had to get him home because it was getting quite late for Tony to be up and that maybe we could see each other again one day. I said yes to her, because I thought she was really nice and she was so honest with me about Tony. You don't find honesty like that these days, I gave her a kiss good night and that was it, she had gone. Marty's girl Vicky was staying the night at Karen's house, which was a minute or so up the road, so she left the party to. That was it; we thought we wouldn't see them again. We carried on drinking and talking about what might have been and thought it was just as well as we were going to Australia and it was paid for and a girl couldn't get in the way of that, or we would lose all our money. We had promised each other that if a girl came on the scene we could not let her stop us from going.

The next morning was lovely and sunny, which helped with the slight hang over I had. Marty and me had breakfast, a bowl of cereal and a cup of tea with Andrew, Martins cousin, we then helped put the living room furniture back into position and picked up glasses half full of drink and just generally had a tidy up. One of Karen's friends who was also at the party had been sent down by Karen to invite the pair of us up the road to her place for a cup of tea, so we could all get to know each other. We said tell Karen thanks but maybe next time. We then said goodbye to martin's auntie and cousins thanked them for having us and made a dash for it. We both liked the girls but just could not get involved with them.

The week that followed I was thinking about Karen quite a lot, she was so nice polite and honest. So I was glad when Marty phoned and said that Karen was trying to get hold of my phone number, well me mum and dads phone number cause I was still at home, and was it all right to give it to her. (She had got Marty's number off of his auntie Janet) " Yer ok mate" I said and within 10 min's Karen was on the phone asking me if I would go out with her on the Saturday... "Oh sorry I can't I'm really busy this Saturday but maybe next Saturday we could go to the cinema", I said to her. Karen said "ok" and it was settled. I was taking another girl out this Saturday, that's why I was to busy. It was arranged before I went to Janet's party the week before.

A week or so had passed and Saturday came. The girl I took out the previous Saturday was a nice girl, but I kept on thinking about Karen.

We had arranged to pick both Vicky and Karen up from Karen's House in Wexham near Slough and on the way there I said to Marty "We were pretty pissed up the night of your auntie's party, I hope the girls look the same as remember them ".

We pulled up outside Karen's house in Martin's white cortina estate that he had bought off of his dad cheap. Marty parked up and before he could turn off the engine Karen had opened the front door of her house. She was standing there with one hand holding the door open and the other hand on the collar of her bloody great German shepherd dog called Prince, but Karen looked beautiful, I actually didn't give a lot of thought to the dog barking away, I was just so happy that she was even better than I had imagined her from the party. As we went in Martin saw Vicky and was happy with the way she looked to, they both looked very lovely.

It was quite tough for the girl's on that first date as it was also my dad's 50th birthday and they were having a BBQ for friends and family at my parent's house. So some time during the night we had to pop in and show our faces. We stayed for about two hours at me mum and dad's then the four of us went to the cinema and then on for a drink. The only thing on that weekend at the cinema was Universal Soldier with (Jean-Claude Van Damme) in it. It's an action movie not what the girls wanted to see but we ended up seeing it anyway, well most of it I think Karen had other things on her mind, I know I did.

At the end of the night Karen offered us all to stay at her house the night and as Tony was being looked after by Marty's auntie Janet. We thought it was a great idea and Marty didn't say no either.

We started seeing the girls quite often, every weekend I would stay with Karen and

34

she would do a roast dinner for Martin and me every Sunday. It was great I would be at home with mum and dad during the week and from Friday night I was with Karen and Tony. Being apart during the week really made us want to see each other at the weekends. Don't ask about Martin, I think at one stage he was seeing three girls at the same time at this point and things didn't last with him and Vicky. It wasn't going to last much longer with Karen and me either as Australia was getting closer and the thought of leaving Karen was very bad. We really started to love each other over the last 9 months and going to Australia for (I don't know how long) was going to be tough on us both.

Two weeks before we went I took Karen and Tony down to the coast for a week to a place called West Wittering, where we stayed in a caravan. There's not much to do there for a 9-year-old boy but we all had a good time and became even closer. It turned out to be the first holiday Karen and Tony had ever been on and I promised Karen that it wouldn't be the last we go on together.

CHAPTER 5

Departure day...

The day had come for Martin and I to go to Australia for the second time. The date was 20th of June 1993,one day after my 23rd birthday. Karen and Tony had stayed with me at my mum and dads house the previous night. This was going to be one of the hardest things that I had ever done, saying goodbye to a woman that I had only known for about 9 month's but who I new I wanted to spend the rest of my life with.

I only had a single bed at my parent's house but that would be enough as the way we felt about each other the closer the better.

I woke up the next morning with the sun shining through my bedroom window but it was still very early, Karen's head was on my chest and my arm was around her.

If I could of got out of going I would have but it was all paid for and I could not let Martin down.

It was an early flight that we were on, about nine'ish and we had to be at the airport about an hour or two before, so it didn't give us a lot of time in the morning, which was good, because if I had to wait until the afternoon I may not have gone at all. Karen was so brave she had held back the tears up until the point of going, and when I had to leave the house I started as well. And not once had she told me not to go, she just wanted me to get it out of my system and then come back and spend the rest of my life with her. We cuddled I said goodbye to Tony and I got into my brother's car and we set off up the road. I was very tearful all the way to the airport, with Wayne bless him assuring me that Karen and Tony would be ok and that he would watch out for them while I'm away.

We arrived at the airport to be greeted by Martin and his whole family smiling and joking, they could probably see that I had been crying but I wasn't bothered, I'm just glad I said my goodbyes at home and not here at the airport.

After a bit of friendly chat with everyone Marty and I decided to go to check-in and get rid of our big bags. We only ever travelled with two bags one with clothes and bits in and one hand luggage, this was so that we could keep track of our stuff easier and with all the travelling across Australia, if you had to rush anywhere you just picked your bag up and you were off, as Martin could vouch for when we had to run for a Greyhound bus when we were staying in Cairns Queensland.

At check-in Marty said to me that he thought it might have been a bit touch and go if I was going to turn up. I said that it was a bit touch and go, but I couldn't let him down. After all just say I didn't go and Karen and I split up a month later I would have regretted it big time.

We finally settled on the plane after saying our goodbyes to Martins family and me brother Wayne, a Qantas jumbo jet; next stop Singapore for 4 days.

We had spent 10 hours at Singapore last time we went to Australia and liked it so much that we promised ourselves next time we would stay, so we were going to.

After a very long flight we finally arrived at Singapore and this time we were staying. A Shaffer driven Mercedes that belonged to the hotel we were about to stay in picked us up at Singapore airport, and took us straight to the hotel, it was lovely we were on the 16th floor and their was a pool on about the 5th floor. Weather was great as usual in Singapore and we couldn't have asked for a better trip. But despite all the luxury's I still thought about Karen every minute, and every so often I would work out the time difference back home and wonder what Karen was up to at that precise minute. I was keeping my thoughts to myself though so I didn't spoil this exciting time for Marty.

This trip was a bit different from before, we were to land at Adelaide and not Perth as before and we were going to be greeted by one of my dad's cousins Ray whom I had never met and my dad had not seen for 30 years so we were all strangers really.

Dad used to keep in touch by writing to him every so often and it was in one of dad's letters that dad had asked if we could visit for a week or two.

We did eventually arrive in Adelaide nearly a week after setting off from England. It was late about 11pm at night and all I could think about was poor Ray not only was he good enough to take us in for two weeks and didn't even know us but now we were making him wait at Adelaide airport this late during the week.

We got off the plane and went straight for our bag's at the baggage terminal trying to be as quick as possible for Ray's sake. Going through customs they singled Marty and I out and wanted to check our bags. This wasn't like before when we had work permits, which would last a year, this time we had open holiday tickets and 6 month visas which prohibited us from working. This wasn't our fault this was their procedures. You could ask for an extension but you had to prove you had enough funds to support yourself for the duration of your trip without working.

The customs guys started going through our bags and they came across some of my certificates, which I had achieved whilst training as a painter and decorator when I was on the Y.T.S.

From that moment on me and Marty were taken into separate rooms and questioned, I was told that if I said anything that contradicted what Martin had said we would be on the next flight home.

They wanted to know why I had trade certificates in my bag when it was prohibited for me to work.

At this stage I was doing my best to think about what Marty was answering but also at the back of my mind I was thinking this was my get out, I could go back home on the next flight and see Karen and it wouldn't look as though I let Martin down. I felt bad for Ray who had been waiting all this time to pick us up. The rest of the flight had long gone and it was getting to the early hours of the morning by now. They even questioned poor Ray waiting outside to see what his connection to us was, and as he had never met me and I had never met him it didn't look too good for us. I had said that the certificates were in my bag for an emergency, in case we ran out of money I could do a bit of work to get some money to get back to the airport. I don't know if they believed that but the fact that we had over $6000 dollars on us each eased their fears a bit, we had enough cash to see us through our stay. $6000 dollars sounds a lot but it worked out to about £2.700 English pounds, which both Marty and I had worked very hard for. They finally let us go but our cards were marked and they were going to make sure that we returned.

When we finally met Ray he was a great bloke we apologised for the delay and went back to his place for a cup of tea and a long sleep.

We stayed with Ray and his lovely family for a great 2 weeks they took us to loads of places including the casino, we then moved on to Marty's relatives who lived in Dandenong near Frankston, Melbourne way.

Marty's brother Danny had left for Australia 2 months before us and was also staying with his relatives in Dandenong. So we all stayed there a couple of weeks then the three of us started travelling up the east coast of Australia for the trip of a lifetime.

We stayed at Kings Cross in Sydney and saw the opera house and went down Sydney Harbour where we took a cruise under Sydney Harbour Bridge, from there we went on to Surfers Paradise where we stayed a week in a back packers lodge. Then a short 1day stay in Brisban then on to our final destination Cairns.

While in Cairns we rented an apartment for one month and used it as a base and somewhere to leave our bags while we went and done different things.

The three of us went diving on the Great Barrier Reef. What an experience that was. People in England said to us that we would need diving certificates before they would let us dive, but this was Australia and when we went on our trip on the reef they said that they supplied all wet suits and diving equipment so if anyone wanted to dive they could. They would let them hang onto the anchor chain of the boat under the water and if you were breathing ok with the oxygen and wanted to go for a swim around the reef just give them the ok sign and they would take you on a guided swim, if you felt uneasy under the water with the oxygen just give them the no go sign and they would take you back up. So that's what we did.

Just before we got all the oxygen tanks on and went for our dive, the crew of the ship told us what to expect and what we were going to see down there and that there was this huge sea bass called Oscar and that he was used to divers and always came up to the divers for a look, it was used to visitors in it's domain daily and so were the reef sharks. Even though the sharks could probably take a hand or foot off, they stay mainly on the bottom and have never given them any hassle.

There's that word again *shark,* 20ft great whites and the Jaws theme always spring to mind. At this point a sea bass seemed completely irrelevant.

We done our stint holding on to the anchor chain gave them the ok and off we went. The colours down on the reef were truly breath taking and me and Marty were in complete amazement at the beauty of it all, even the reef sharks seemed so graceful moving in and out of the coral. It's at this point when your mind is trying to take everything in when lo and be hold the so called irrelevant sea bass Oscar swims by, now I don't know if it was just me but this thing was huge and up close it looked like a bloody whale it did shit me up a bit.

We had a barbeque on the boat on the way home and I even bought a video of Marty and me scuba diving on the reef with Oscar.

We used our apartment at Cairns as a base then done as much as we could.

We stayed at a place called Palm Cove for 1 week, which was absolutely beautiful full of palm trees on a golden sandy beach; we also stayed in a tropical rain forest at a little village called Crocodylus Village with natural water falls, also picture perfect we went white water rafting also.

Oh and their was Danny's attempt at bungee jumping. I say attempt because Danny had wanted to do this for weeks and kept trying to persuade me and Marty to do it aswel. Now we were actually at the site, it was apparent just how high this bungee really was. Danny gets weighed in at the weigh point at the bottom and then we get given the ok to go up. Marty and me were also allowed to go up to watch him; It was a very long way up, I started getting that tingly feeling in my legs, the higher we were going the worse it was getting. We finally made it to the top and you could see for miles. These guys call Danny over to the edge and started to fasten him up then told him where to stand for his big jump. There were hundreds of people at the bottom standing and sitting around this lake and a boat ready to grab you after your slight dunk into the water headfirst. So here he is right on the edge, the point of no return, the safety guys say, "Right when you are ready then, jump straight out and go". I had never seen Danny so white, he does this funny little movement with his legs and we think he is about to go and that's it he is still there, " I can't do it" he says. Ok come away from the edge compose yourself and try again they say to him. So Danny takes a few deep breaths turns looks at Marty, who has his hands over his face trying not to show Danny the laugh that had just come over him, then he approaches the edge again. By this time people are shouting from the bottom "come on jump" the guys say to Danny "look just don't look down look straight ahead and jump". Another little wobble and wiggle and nothing, "no I can't sorry" Dan says "ok come back we'll un-tie you and you can go back down". While they were un-tying Danny one of the safety guys says to Marty and me that they had been on a good run, everyone was going of the edge first time up until now, once one refuses to jump it starts the others off.

We got the mini bus back to Cairns and went back to our apartment and got ready for our usual night at the End of the World. It was a nightclub that used to serve food if you got in before 6pm and you only had to pay for your entry in to the club, which was about 6 bucks, and food was free. They used to have theme nights especially for back packers.

It seems really weird but I swear I saw 2 girls in that club that I used to know from back home when I was growing up, we used to live in the same street. But when you are half way round the world and in a nightclub in Cairns it's hard to justify they are the same people I mean what are the odds. The only regret I have is that I didn't go up to them and find out, they were with other guys and I didn't want to spoil things for them. So if that was you Maria and Saffron I did see you both in Cairns in that nightclub and I'm sorry I didn't say hello.

We had been in Australia for nearly 5 months by now and we had seen most of the east coast this time. So now we had done every part of Australia and we'd been to

Phillip Island aswel. We had flown in helicopters, little four seated aeroplanes been white water rafting, scuba diving on the reef and so much more but now I wanted to go back to my Karen.

Two years previous we started at Perth went up the west coast across to Katherine down the middle to Alice Springs down to Adelaide then over to Melbourne then back to Adelaide across the Nullabor Plain to Kalgoorlie then back to Perth. This time we started at Adelaide went over to Melbourne up the East coast to Sydney then Brisbane then on to Cairns and back to Melbourne. Not bad considering we were both 23 years old.

We decided between the 3 of us that we would start heading back I was aiming to get home for Christmas to be with Karen and the Family. So it was on the Greyhound bus back to Melbourne to stay with Marty's cousin until we decided to leave.

Danny Martin's brother left first then I left three weeks later at the end of November and Marty left in the New Year and had his second Christmas in Australia.

CHAPTER 6

*T*ogether again...

This is going to be a hard chapter, as I will be putting a lot of myself and my emotions into this one, so here goes.

We touched down at Heathrow Airport and as I looked out of the plane window I could see yet another dull and rainy November in England. A part of me is saying what the hell am I doing back here I just left the Australian summer for this and another part of me is saying how much I am looking forward to seeing Karen.

I knew Karen was worth the sacrifice of sun and surf, I could always go again one day but I may never find another Karen. I loved this girl and there wasn't one day in the 5 months I had been away that I hadn't thought about her.

When I finally got through customs and into the arrivals area I heard this scream and saw Karen running towards me it was lovely. Wayne and me dad were there to meet me to.

No B.M.W. this time, Wayne was picking me up in a work van and Karen and I sat cuddling up in the back amongst the dust and tools. It felt so natural being with her.

We got Christmas out of the way and then I got a job at an electronics company in Binfield near Bracknell, they specialised in electronic hand held bar code scanners. I was doing odd jobs for them such as painting and doing deliveries of their equipment all over the country. It was only supposed to be for a few months but I started taking an interest in their equipment and then they got me working on it, a bit of soldering here and there replacing components and chips and before I knew it they were paying for me to do a course at college.

I had been there about 5 months and then Karen got pregnant. I couldn't believe it, Karen phoned me up at my mum and dads house and told me and I was over the moon. I was going to be a dad and Tony was going to have a brother or sister, I had a smile on my face all night just like when I passed my driving test. I knew that I had to knuckle down and try and keep this job as we were going to be a bigger family.

Karen and I weren't actually living together yet as she was on income support and if I moved in permanently she could lose this money and I wasn't earning enough to support us all yet. So I was seeing her at weekends and Wednesday nights. At this stage I only had a draw with a few clothes in at her house but it was lovely, as being away from each other a few days just made us want each other more, we even wrote to each other on the days we weren't together. I even wrote a letter to Karen the night she told me I was going to be a dad, just to say how much I loved her and how happy I was.

I always knew even from a very young age that I was quite a deep person and that once I found the right girl I would stay with her for good and Karen was that girl, I just hoped she wanted to be with me for good.

Tony was approaching 12 and was now at senior school Karen had moved to a place called Cippenham near Slough and we'd had our baby daughter in November 1994, we named her Danielle Louise Harding.

Things were getting tougher now, I did eventually move in with Karen and Tony, but he was becoming a bit of a handful, some times I was coming home from work and going straight to the police station to pick him up, I was taking him to football practice during the week and football at weekends to play for the club he belonged to and we even got him into Windsor Slough and Eton athletics club for one season as they saw a bit of potential in him, when they done a visit to his school. But it didn't matter what we did it wasn't good enough. Going out with his mates and getting into trouble and smoking seemed better, Tony had lost interest in going to athletics and football.

The next few years were quite tough, especially for me. As I wasn't Tony's real dad it was very hard for me to tell him off and when Karen did he didn't take any notice, I used to wait until things were getting so bad or he had made Karen cry before I would step in because I wanted Karen to sort things out with her son, she had done it before I was there, but they know it all at 15 and 16. When I did tell him off it always ended up unpleasant and awkward for us both, but he never once said to me "you aren't my real dad you can't tell me off", and I think a lot of him for that.

Danielle was growing up beautifully but we still had problems with Tony, it was putting a lot of pressure on Karen and me. We had moved house again to get more room, still in the same area but into a bigger house 3 bedrooms. Then Karen and me decided that we were going to give Tony one last chance. He was about to leave school so we decided that if he got into any more trouble we would move out of the area. The police had told us that things will go one of two ways, he will either carry on getting into trouble and wind up inside or he will get it out of his system and quieten down himself, which was a risk. It was a risk that we weren't going to take so in order to keep the family together we told Tony our plans to move, it didn't seem to bother him that much, maybe he thought we were joking about moving as within a week he was in trouble again. Tony didn't have to change school, cause we made sure he had properly left (see we still thought of him) but they don't think that you do. So we stuck to our word and started looking for a council exchange in Bracknell. He doesn't know anyone over there and maybe he can start a fresh.

By this time we had our second daughter Rebecca Sarah Harding, born in May 1999.

It was a big step for Karen moving out of the area, all her friends and her mum lived in Slough, her dad had died when she was just 16 and her mum was in a wheel chair still living over Slough way. Her mum had taken her dad's death quite hard as anyone would but it just put more pressure on Karen. Karen had no brothers or sisters so from 16 she was looking after her mum and her baby Tony with very little help.

Now we live in Bracknell further from Karen's Family but closer to mine. At first Karen didn't want to be in Bracknell not because of the area but the state of the house we had moved into. To say it was bad was an understatement, Karen was crying for 2 weeks, as we had just finished decorating our previous house and now we had to start again. I actually took film of the house and sent it to my local MP because I could not believe a council housing inspector had agreed for us to move into the house being in the state it was in. The guy who previously lived there even took the cat flap with him when he left so we had a 1ft square hole in the back door in the middle of November and with two little girls and Tony, my priority was to keep them all warm.

Tony was now away from what was pulling him down in Slough and was now at home with us with nothing to do, so I managed to get him a job at the same company I worked for and he quickly realised that if you want things in life you have to work for them, so he did. Yes he still had his moments but now he worked with adults and being in that environment made him grow up quicker.

Tony is now 27 at the time I wrote this, self-employed with two beautiful children of his own who are of course my grandchildren. And Karen and me are very proud of him.

We moved from that house after about 8 months we re-decorated it then moved on to a different part of Bracknell cause it didn't matter what I did to the place Karen wasn't happy there and where we moved to was right next door to some friends that we had known since I was a kid, great people both sides of us.

We also have another son now Adam Stephen Harding, who at the time of writing this is 5 years old, Danielle is now 15 and Rebecca 10 me well I'm still Karen's toy boy cause Karen is 5 years older than me… you work it out.

I still love Karen as much now as when I first met her, no actually more, I tell her and the kids I love them every day and I always will.

I see Marty regularly and yes he still has the gift of the gab. He now has a daughter Named Holly and we all get together and take the kids out quite often.

CHAPTER 7

Now I Know...

Well after all the exercising I have done over the last 15 years, although it has kept me lean it doesn't matter how much I do if I don't keep it up regularly my body wants to revert back to it's happy state, which is what I call it. It's the condition it likes best and 10 days is about the complete revert, which means that if you don't exercise again within 10 days it's like starting from the beginning again. Mind you with the aches and pains I have it makes me wonder how much is caused by exercise. Then again I do over do it sometimes. I reckon just having an active job like on a building site would be enough for the body to stay in shape but a lot does depend on genes and diet.

My main reason for keeping fit is to be active in later life not only for me but for the kids to, I have promised the kids that I will still do 10 pull-ups when I'm 70 years old. I'm 39 when writing this and still feel very fit, I still feel as I did in my early 20's but with a few more aches and pains and with grey in my hair, "yes" I still do have the thin bit in the middle from when I used to pull it out, but like I said with age it looks more natural.

Mentally as I have got older although I have more confidence in my thinking I still can not get my head round why some of the smartest people lack the simplest thing, common sense. Maybe it's me, I'm left handed and us lefty's think with the opposite side of the brain and I have on a number of occasions looked at a situation from totally the opposite to other people. Being left handed is very important to me and has definitely ruled my life and the way I think. For instance nearly everything is made for right handed people, which means we either try to do it with our left hand or adapt and do it with our rights, and this has made me very ambidextrous and when my son Adam was about three he used to colour with both hands and when we ask him which hand he likes to write with he says both. So me being if you like forced to be ambidextrous over the years has had a bit of a gene pull on to Adam.

Just recently I attended 3 funerals in 4 weeks 2 friends and a family member. Karen's mum Catherine, who died at the age of 83, bless her. We did get her over to Bracknell for the last few years of her life and she was able to see all the children regularly. But although death is all around you on TV and in the papers you never really think about it until it's close to home. It makes you realise that anything could happen to anyone at any time and never forget that. Life is a precious thing and it has made me think of my own life, have I wasted it.

If you could come back as anyone else who would it be? A great athlete, a pop star or movie star, scientist, doctor, pilot, who? Think about it for a second. From a young age my answer has been the same person all the time…me! Why, because I know what I've put into my body I know what it can take and the way I think. Alright I am no genius, far from it but I like me, I don't mean I love myself I mean I like the fact that I exercise and watch what I eat and the colours I like and the films I like. You may think I'm a nutter because I like to run but that's me it's part of me, my children also love running that's who we are, my friend and his family hate sports but between them they can play about six different instruments they were brought up on music and instruments and that's who they are and what they do.

I don't know if it's the same for everyone but when I reached my thirty's thing's seemed to be a lot clearer in my head I could learn thing's quicker and I could sort of tell what was round life's corners before it happened and writing seemed easy, whether I was any good or not didn't matter to me, I liked to write. It was like everything I had learnt in life such as travelling, relationships, children, sickness, religion, death, work, everything that I had ever learnt has sort of prepared me for the rest of life, how ever long that is.

You know the saying healthy body healthy mind, well it's true as long as I stay healthy I am able to handle things a lot better because I don't feel guilty for the moments that I lounge around and watch TV and pig out a bit and that guilt isn't there when I have to accomplish something.

Just because this is who I am it doesn't mean who you are is any better or worse, you can't change who you are meant to be. Sure I have done things I regret but I'm not going to ponder on those moments, that's been and gone. Just try and be happy with whom you are and if you aren't then try to change things one at a time, cause you may not be here tomorrow. You can read my philosophy on life and the way I see it further on in the book.

I'm nearly 40 now and I'm already a dad, granddad, godfather and an uncle. I run, and enter about 5 or 6 10k road races a year sometimes for charity sometimes for fitness, you may see me at one of the races, if you do say hello. I also go shooting when I can and try to spend as much time with the kids as possible or involve them in what I'm doing. "Don't I kids".

Some of my happiest moments have been with my children. I was at the birth of all of them, and would tell any man not to miss the birth of their children.

One of the saddest points for me in the children growing up is when they stop calling me daddy and start calling me dad.

As regard to exercising, there is hard ways of doing things and easy ways of doing things: Take 300 press-ups for instance, they could be done in 20's, 30's or what ever you liked, but remember the more you do each go the longer your recovery rate and the tireder you get between sets, which means it could take 2 or three hours to do 300 press-ups if done properly. But there's another way, 5 press-ups a minute for an hour will achieve 300 and will have the same or better effect on your body as you are doing them in a fraction of the time and your recovery rate is equal every set.

Whatever exercises you do, have a think about them for a while, you may be wasting time and energy on something that could be done more effectively or done a different way.

That's about it now; I have said almost all I have to say up to this point in my life Now you have this book you have something to compare with, you can see all the different exercises I have done to stay physically and mentally fit. I don't know how long I can keep exercising to this standard but I will keep going until my body doesn't let me, but if I live a long life I am determined to still do the 10 pull up's in my 70's.

My fitness diary does go on a bit so I apologise now if you get bored with it but I had to put it in for my granddad.

" This is Me" Love you all loads... I wonder what the rest of life has in store.

<u>Vital Statistics</u>

Favourite films: Warriors, Platoon, Braveheart, Great Escape, Ben Hur, Aliens, Jaws

Favourite comedy: Only Fools and Horses, Red Dwarf

Favourite music group: INXS, ABBA, Aerosmith, Bee Gees, and lots more.

Favourite comedian/funny man: Norman Wisdom

Favourite colour: Purple

Favourite sport: Athletics

Favourite car: Porsche 911

Favourite food/meal: Roast Dinner, Pasta, Rice, Fish and Chicken

Favourite alcoholic drink: Jack Daniels and coke, Pear Cider

Favourite soft drink: Blackcurrant

Favourite month: May

Toddler saves friend in fire

BURNHAM BOY DRAGGED OUT — BY HIS HAIR

A FOUR-YEAR-OLD toddler who had crawled underneath a blazing bed was saved by his three-year-old friend who dragged him out by his hair.

Stephen Harding, who is still shaken by the fire, dived into action to save his friend David _____ from a blazing bedroom and togther with four year old Michael _____ they made a rush for safety.

The drama started at David's home at The Green, Burnham, when the toddlers started to play with matches upstairs and set alight to two beds.

Luckily, a mystery person spotted smoke coming from the bedroom and phoned the fire brigade before too much damage was caused.

Mrs _____ saw the blaze when she returned from a 10 minute visit about 50 yards up the road to her mother.

Her husband, Mr _____, 37, said: "All I know is that my son David, his friend and another little girl used a broom handle to unhook the spare key we keep by the door.

"They went upstairs and set light to the two beds with matches. I don't know where they got them from. They are not the ones I use."

Mr _____ has appealed for the person who phoned the brigade to come forward so he can thank him.

"We were very lucky," he admitted. "Thing is I keep my best suit under the mattress."

Stephen . . . saved friend by his hair.

Above: The News Paper cutting mum and dad kept of me after the fire.

Below: Dad and me, as you can see I was still pulling my hair out at age 12.

54

Marty and me on top of Ayres Rock, in 1990 with the Olga's Rock formation in the background.

Above: In Cairns. Danny, Martins brother all strapped up for the bungee jump he didn't do.

Below: Danny and Me just finished diving the Great Barrier Reef.

Above: me running the 10k Sam Run in 2005.

Below: Danielle being presented with her third place trophy by the Mayor in 2008.

Karen in 2008, just about to make a cup of tea.

Rebecca on the log flume at Hayling Island, summer 2008.

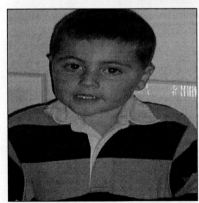

Adam in 2008

Short Stories

The Golf Course

When I first met Karen it was very clear to me that she had a thing about Gary Lineker, (he's a footballer if you didn't know). She had posters of him on her bedroom walls mugs with his head on and little footballs with his name and picture on. I remember I drew a moustache on his poster that she had on her bedroom wall and Karen didn't speak to Marty or me for a day, funny though...

I would go over to see her at Wexham on a Saturday morning and at 12 o'clock mid day Karen would be sitting in front of the TV with the remote control in her hand waiting for Gary Lineker to report on all the latest football news. She would have a video in the machine ready to record him. When I say him I mean him. Gary would have a team of experts in the studio with him talking about football and when ever Gary would ask a question Karen would press record and as soon as the camera panned away from Gary and on to one of his experts for a reply Karen would press pause, so by the time it had finished she had a tape full of Gary Lineker asking questions and getting no answers coming back. Karen had loads of tapes like this; actually I think she has still got them somewhere.

Karen also liked Rob Lowe, John Travolta and a few others but none compared to Gary.

I have never got jealous or envious of anyone, I don't know why it just doesn't bother me what others have or who they are, which is just as well with Karen and her Gary thing. I found out about Gary Lineker doing a celebrity golf thing at some golf course near Burnham/Slough, it wasn't publicised and very low key so I decided on the Sunday Gary was playing I would surprise Karen and take her to the course and see if she could see him in the flesh for the first time.

We pulled into the Golf course on the Sunday morning, it was a lovely sunny day, a nice gravel drive and all these fancy and expensive cars in the car park and I parked up in an old Montego estate, which was a company car, it wasn't bad and ideal for us not only did we have Tony but we had Danielle as well and her pushchair and everything else that went with a young baby went straight into the boot. By now I had told Karen what we were doing at the golf course and her face was a glow.

We all got out of the car trying not to arouse suspicion, I pulled Danielle's folded up pushchair out of the boot pretending it was a set of golf clubs then slowly shut the boot as if we were supposed to be there. I got Danielle quickly strapped into the pushchair and thought what the hell do we do now. Karen was like an owl; I swear her head went 360 degrees looking for Gary. As luck would have it I could see through this bit of woodland and straight onto the golf course and I could see people on a fairway playing there next shot to the pin. I looked further back down the fairway and onto the tee and would you credit it there he was Gary Lineker with other golfers just teeing up ready to play the hole that we could see. What bloody good timing, it was like it was meant to be. I told Karen that I think I saw Gary Lineker on the tee over there through the woods and before I could get a response she was gone through the woods and onto the course. The lying cow, she told me she couldn't run; well she was doing a bloody good impression now. "Hold on" I shouted as I tried to get into the woods pushing the pushchair but she was gone, I could see Karen running along the side of the fairway towards the tee with pen and paper in hand for his autograph, oh my god I thought, it was like watching a streaker on match of the day. She gets up to him and watches him take his tee shot onto the fairway, then starts following him up the fairway towards his ball. Bloody hell we are going to get done here I thought, my girlfriend on the fairway following Gary Lineker and me watching from the woods with a baby in a pushchair, it didn't look to good, especially when the next lot of golfers came on to the same hole they did give me some strange looks.

It wasn't long before Karen went out of view, only because the hole they were playing had a bend to the left or a dog leg left as they call it, and with the club house in the way all I could do was go back to the car strap Danielle into her car seat and get ready for a quick get away, cause god knows what Karen will get up to, and I didn't have a clue how long she was going to be. Please don't let her follow that poor man round every hole I was thinking to myself. Next minute Karen comes walking from behind the club house with a smile from ear to ear, she gets into the car and says "I don't believe it, I actually met him", " I thought I'd lost you for ever there for a minute" I said to her "what did you say to him" I said to Karen as I was driving down the track out of the golf course. "I said that I had been waiting years for this moment" "and what did he say to that" I said to Karen, while keeping me eyes on the road. He said, "not here I hope". I laughed,

Karen proceeded to tell me how nice he was all the way home, and to see her that excited was really great.

Amsterdam

Seven of us went to Amsterdam on a boy's weekend. There was my brothers Wayne and Darren and of course Marty and his brother Danny, our friend Mark who sadly died a couple of years later and Garry another friend.

I'm going to cut this story right down as so much went on over that weekend I'm just going to tell you what happened to me.

As you know Amsterdam is famous for it's red light district. Well you didn't think I was going to talk about windmills and clogs did ya'.

While we were walking round the red light district and having a look in the many offerings in the windows that were lit up, we would pass strip clubs. Now with the ego's going there's only so many strip clubs you can pass without eventually going into one, so we all decided that the next one we pass we were going in and that is exactly what we did.

Up the steps we go past the guy's on the door beckoning us in and over to the window to pay the girl. The girl taking the cash was young and didn't have much on in the way of clothing and I half expected to see her on the stage after she took the money off us to get in, it looked like that when she wasn't performing on stage she was at the front desk taking the money.

"Along the corridor and through the door on the left" she said to us all. I was first through the door and saw it was absolutely full of people watching this couple having sex on the stage, normally you only got to see a couple of birds strip and that was it but over here it was everything, you got your moneys worth here. I looked around for some seats. Although the stage was lit up lovely it was bloody dark along the rows of

63

seats but I could see a whole row free at the front right near the stage, so I said "come on lad's there's seats at the front" and as I started to make my way the rest of the guy's followed. While I was sitting there waiting for the couple to finish their act on the stage and waiting for the next act to come on, I couldn't help wonder why all those blokes were standing up at the back when all these seats were free at the front. Then it suddenly dawned on me, "What twats we are" I said to Marty "these seats were free for a reason" "yes well we did think that but we just followed you" Marty said to me under a whispered voice. I could hear Gary and Danny laughing and commenting about the position we were sitting in, like lambs to the slaughter. When the next act came on and this big coloured lady came out dancing with a banana right in front of us, the words *oh shit* seemed to be whispered by all of us at the same time and the emotions of horror and humour came over us. Laughing at the thought that this woman may pick on one of us and what a laugh it would be if it was one of your mates and the sheer terror that it might be you. Our suspicions where right she actually came off the stage and started dancing in the little space between our legs and the front of the stage, she wiggled straight past me and started to head further down the front row, the relief that she had passed me was great and I looked at Marty and Wayne as she passed them and I could see them laughing with relief to.

Then she stopped and asked some guy to get onto the stage and start dancing, the guy was a bit reluctant at first but he then got up and got onto the stage and was up there dancing like a good'n. Then she preceded back along the front row gyrating towards us again, oh shit I thought one of us I going to get it. She stopped in front of me "on the stage and start dancing" she said to me with a foreign accent, "no way I said" and She repeated, "get on the stage lover boy" "no I'm not getting up there" I said to her again. I looked right and could see the lads laughing, "go on get up there boy" Danny said laughing his head off that I was the one she had targeted. "Ok just stand up then" she said "why" I said looking up to her from my seat while she was waving this banana around, "I'm not going till you stand up, look I will put the banana down" she said and she placed it on the stage behind her. Ok I thought what harm could it do just to stand up, so I did. The next minute she had her arms around me lifted me up turned round and pushed me onto the stage. Now I was up there in front of the lights with this other bloke. I started dancing waiting my fate, I could see the silhouette of all the crowd and just make out the lad's on the front row laughing, then the coloured stripper came back on to the stage and started dancing with us to the music, then she goes over to the banana and lay's on the floor in front of us, she opens her legs and in goes the banana, she peeled it back and pointed to the other bloke to go down and take a bite, so he does, the audience gets louder with laughter now. She then beckoned me "come on you to", so I went over and got into position to take a bite and just as my teeth had clamped round to take a chunk off, her hands go round the back of my head and she forces my head down rolling my face right in between her legs. I came up with banana on my chin and nose you had to see the funny side it was hilarious. Everyone rolled up, we went back to our seats and continued to watch some other acts, and then we went back out into the night knowing that if there are ever any spare seats at the front of any other strip club we won't be sitting in them...

The New Forest

I once went camping to the new forest with a bunch of work colleagues in 1987. It was a very cold October, we all went down in two sherpa mini buses packed with camping equipment, it was supposed to be a company team building exercise, socialising with other work mates on an orienteering sort of thing, "Yer right" company piss up more like.

We got down there at about 11am, the drivers of each van were the supervisors Ken and Fred and responsible for all the tasks that were ahead of us for the week we were down there. Fortunately for us they liked a drink or two. We found our pitch amongst the horse shite and bushes and parked up. "Right we'll put the tents up get sorted out then wip into town and go to the off licence for a few beers, right", Said Ken. "Yes" we all shouted. You'd never seen tents go up so quick. I had a small two man tent which I took along, but I wasn't intending to sleep in it, I took it along for some of the smaller chaps as I'm 6.ft 1 and always found it a bit of a squeeze. I thought I would kip in the big tent that belonged to the company as it had plenty of room.

We took both vans into town and got there about half two. We filled them with beer and wine, then got back and started a fire and prepared for the long cold night ahead. We all got our seats round the fire and started on the drink and having a laugh. By about 9.30pm we were all well on the way, Ken was on the wine straight out of the bottle the way he liked it, and Fred the other supervisor was well into the crate of beer he had bought earlier.

It was pitch black in the forest and the only bit of light we had was coming from the fire, it made it better though, you could just make out who you were talking to through the flames. As the night went on you would speak to someone and get no answer, they were either to pissed to respond or gone for a pee, I was chatting to ken for a bit, then went to the back of one of the vans to get him and me a few more drinks as we were getting a bit low low, Fred was asleep in the van sparko he was well gone and was using the crates of beer with a jumper on top of them as a pillow. He was sort of guarding the drink so we all went steady and had enough for the rest of the week, bless him, doing his supervisory bit, it didn't bloody stop him having a skinful though, but the thought was there. I went back to the fire and what was left of the lads with half a crate of beer, leaving Fred with a decidedly lower pillow, I shouted over to Ken and got no answer, so I edged my way round the fire and no Ken, I looked around and shouted into the darkness just in case he had gone for a pee and taken a stumble, then I saw his little camping chair on its side, then I looked directly behind it and saw two feet coming out of a thorn bush, I poked my head over and looked down at him laughing me head off at the thought of him taking a swig from his bottle of wine and going over into the bush, it took a few seconds for my eyes to adjust to see that he was lying there eyes wide open looking up at the stars, "fucking dark aint it" he said, did I laugh. We got him up and put him back on his perch and he carried on drinking. By about 12 o clock that night most of the lads were in the tents asleep and as I was feeling a little worse for wear myself, I decided to get me head down, so off I go to the big tent only to find it full. (That's why the sods went to bed early) I thought to myself. My only option was the small tent that I had kindly supplied, so I get in with me sleeping bag and squeeze between Tim and Steve.

We were all sleeping with our clothes on for two reasons, one we were all to pissed to take them off and two it was to bloody cold.

I didn't know how long I'd been asleep, but I know the tent was spinning every time

I moved my head and I was busting for a pee aswel, there was no way I was going to hold it in. It was still bloody cold and pitch black, but I just had to pee, got out of my sleeping bag and crawled to the zip of the tent and opened the flap, there was no way I was going out there it was bloody freezing so I got me todger out pocked it out into the night and pissed for what seemed like forever. For a minute there I thought the puddle was going to come back into the tent. I zip up the tent and snuggled back into me sleeping bag then into oblivion.

Next time I wake up its light, I can hear a few of the lads complaining of hangovers and Tim and Steve talking over me in the tent not knowing I'm awake. Then Steve decides to get up and crawls to the front of the tent, he putt's his shoes on and unzips the tent flap and proceeds on all fours through the tiny flap. All of a sudden he shouts out "aaahhr! For fuck sake who's spilt beer here". For a second I thought that some body had, but then I remember my twilight stint, and did I laugh. What he now had on his hands and knees was piss, but I didn't tell him that.

I could have written a book about just that trip, like the time we came back from a hike and found wild horses in our tent eating our food. What a laugh that was seeing grown men trying to get them out of the tent with a carrot, when they're tucking into a feast inside the tent.

Knowing Myself

Through my life I have come to know myself physically and mentally quite well, and will go on finding out and learning about myself until I die.

On the road to me knowing myself and understanding the human race, I have done what I call *minor experiments* on myself, I can only speak for myself and how things have affected my mind and body. It is up to each individual to get to know his or her self and to find out in his or her own way how things will affect them, as what is good for one person may not be good for another.

When I was a youth and in my teens I used to suffer with mouth ulcers. I have always been very active and never had much sleep at the best of times, so people used to say I was run down. I tried all the old remedies, from salt water to gargling with vinegar and hot water, but nothing would shift them for long, so I thought it would be just a part of life for me, I wasn't going to slow down for anyone or anything.

I was once reading my fitness magazine, which I got every once in a while to keep up with all the latest fitness techniques and equipment, when I came across this article about cod liver oil and the properties it has in it and what it can do for the skin and joints. So I started taking them regularly. After about three or four months I suddenly realised that I hadn't had a mouth ulcer for quite a while and could only put it down to the cod liver oil, so I stopped taking them for a couple of weeks and sure enough the ulcers came back. So that was it I had finally found a cure. But not only on my ulcers, if I had bit my lip by accident it would have normally turned into an ulcer but now it just goes.

I take a 1000mg of cod liver oil a day and will carry on taking them until I die, they have also had a remarkable affect on my joints, but I have found that taking less than 1000mg a day reduced their effectiveness.

Maybe they would work on stomach ulcers to!!

Sleep and Dreams

I have always wondered about dreams. I mean how can you dream about things that your brain has never experienced, yet you do.

I generally sleep on my left side and normally have a good night's sleep, but occasionally I would dream or maybe have the odd nightmare. I found that every time I did dream I was lying on my back. So I experimented and found that what makes me dream is the position of my head when I fall asleep. I now know how to lye if I want to dream. Maybe the brain sit's differently or it rests on something, I don't know, but I know that if I lay on my back looking straight up at the ceiling and fall asleep I will dream. The same is true with my wife, so maybe everyone has a certain position in which they can lye in, so they are able to dream.

Religion

What religion is right for you?

I have a lot of relatives that are Jehovah's witnesses and my mum has been baptised a Jehovah's witness, so I know a fair bit about the religion. As a kid I was taught about God their way and naturally you think it's the right way and that all other religion is wrong. Well what I have found is that most people are either born or raised in their religion and know no other way and it doesn't matter what you say about their religion they will defend it to the end, saying their religion is right and everyone else is wrong.

I have had friends in all different religions and each of them tell me the good things About their religion and the bad things about all the others. So I have come to the conclusion that no one religion is 100% right and no one religion is 100% wrong, they all have good bits and bad bits about them and because of this I believe in God my own way, with my whole heart and my whole mind, he knows who is good and who is bad and one day we will all be judged by what we have done in our lives.

My Philosophy's

Never go looking for trouble and try to avoid it if possible.

But if it is unavoidable get in quick and fast, only you can decide whether a confrontation needs to be fought.

Always have 100% confidence in yourself; this does not mean be cocky.

Never quit, even if you fail badly, plod on and overcome.

Try to condition yourself physically and mentally for any situation, be prepared.

Always be yourself, independent. Don't follow others be followed.

Always believe in god, because someone created us

Everyone is so quick to accept evil, ghosts and the devil. But there is an opposite, which is good, love and god.

The bible is the way forward for mankind; believe me.

Second is the first loser.

Make every moment of life count; live for the moment.

Like yourself, like who you are, like the way you express yourself and most of all like the way you think, because what when and how we think, runs our lives.

Like your own company; time with yourself.

If someone takes the Mickey out of you or laughs at you, laugh with them. When they see it doesn't bother you and you don't bite they will soon stop.

Always try to educate yourself even if it's watching a movie, you may hear or see something about life that you never knew. If it's predictable it's not educational.

Always try to help yourself, if you want anything try to get it yourself, try not to rely on others.

Always keep and be active throughout life, as your body will naturally want to slow down with age, always fight it. As soon as you become lazy it becomes worse and you'll start to put on weight and your bones will thin earlier in life.

The grass is never greener elsewhere. Life is life wherever you go, just the scenery changes.

True love is two people being one; nothing can come between one.

Death is always around the corner; *always*

Always try your best at everything you do.

Older people are wiser. Never get wise and clever mixed. Just because someone may be clever at something, to be wise about life is always better. Always respect your elders; wisdom is knowledge.

To be wise about life is being a survivor of life.

"The pen is mightier than the sword" No argument.

Try to be honest with yourself and others. "Honesty is the best policy"

Treat and speak to people, as you would like to be treated or spoken to.

Always be polite, please and thank you never go a miss.

Be wary of everybody; remember the only real person you can trust is yourself

Thieves, liars, bullies, rudeness and laziness, are the 5 worst things a person can have. If you have one or more of these traits someone will always hate you.

Try and help people out if you can. But don't let them take advantage of you, cause once they do they will again.

Always love your partner fully and never have more than one partner. You can't love them both the same. Also you will be falling into one of the five traits; lying.

War is hell; Make the most of your life. You have it easy compared to the men that have fought for their countries and the people that have been tortured for their beliefs.

We moan about our problems and our lives, just think if you lived in a country that was constantly bombed, and you didn't even know if you were going to see the next day. Only one thing would matter to you, *survival.*

Try not to let money motivate you. Your family should always take priority.

A child is closer to perfection than any adult, as they know no language and have no conscious mental thought. They are waiting to be moulded by their loving parents.

Giving is better than receiving.

Don't worry about death, we all die at the moment, it's how we die that you should worry about.

We were created for a life far superior to the one we have, that's why we only use a fraction of our brains capabilities. This is only the beginning of mans existence.

When we are dead we are conscious of nothing, just like being asleep without breathing. It is therefore not death we should fear. But the hoping it's not some horrific way.

As the world goes on people are getting lazier and greedier.

Structurally people are the same; *physically* people can make themselves different; *mentally* we are all different; with all the billions of people on the earth, mentally there are no two people the same. *Human urges*: most of the population are attracted to the opposite sex, just think the urge or attraction of a woman to a man or vice versa, is built into the brain it cannot be controlled it is a natural urge.

But imagine a man or a woman having that same urge to someone of the same sex, the urge is mental, it cannot be controlled, even though the man or woman know its wrong the urge is so strong they cannot stop themselves even thinking about it.

Nobody is perfect, and nobody can control his or her brain to work perfectly.

We would all kill if our lives or our family's lives were in danger. You would be classed as a psychopath to kill for fun, but for survival it would be different.

Same again, the urge for some people to kill is more exciting to them than sex, and so is the same for drugs and so on. Can we be blamed for our urges?
This is why some people have more will power than others, *Example*: if there are two drug users trying to quit, its not the one with the most will power who will succeed, but the one whose urge for the drug is less who will come through.

Will power is driving yourself on through a hardship, like doing something you are not used to doing and having the will and mental strength to do it. There is no urge there at all.

Always be happy with what you've got. There are always people worse off than you, and there will always be people better of than you. As long as you are alive you are better off than someone.

Fitness Training 1995 to 2008

This is when I started to keep a record of the exercises I used to do. As you can see it starts in January 95 and goes on to 2008.

I kept a diary of my exercises so I could keep track of how my body developed with age, and how much my body could physically take before it naturally wanted to slow down.

JANUARY   95

Tue 3rd} stretching and kicks

Sun 8th} 80 press-ups

Mon 9th} 106 pull-ups (80 with weights)

Fri 13th} Bodyworks gym

Sat 14th} 80 press-ups

Sun 15th} 90 press-ups

Mon 16th} 100 pull-ups (80 with weights) also did some stretching and kicks

Sun 22nd} 130press-ups (80+50)

Wed 25th} arm workout also stretching and kick

Fri 27th} arm workout and stretching

Mon 30th} 80 press-ups and a little arms workout

FEBRUARY 95

Thu 2nd} 110 pull-ups with weights, 95 press-ups, 30 leg raises on pull up bar.

Thu 9th} 80 press-ups

Fri 10th} chest and triceps workout

Sun 12th} 70 press-ups

Mon 13th} 100 pull-ups (74 with weights)

Thu 16th} arm workout and stretching, kicks

Mon 20th} 80 pull-ups (with weights) and 30 leg raises

Fri 24th} chest and triceps workout

Sun 26th} went jogging

MARCH 95

Thu 2nd} arms workout

Mon 6th} 70 press-ups, 50 pull-ups (12 with weights), some stretching

Fri 10th} chest and triceps workout

Mon 13th} 80 press-ups

Fri 17th} 100 press-ups in one go

Sun 19th} 80 press-ups

Mon 20th} 100 pull-ups (75 with weights), and 50 press-ups

Fri 24th} chest and triceps workout

Mon 27th} 100 pull-ups, plus stretching and kicks

Tue 28th} 120 press-ups (80+40)

Thu 30th} a little arms workout

Fri 31st} went jogging

APRIL 95

Mon 3rd} 100 pull-ups (74 with weights) also a little arms workout

Tue 4th} stretching and kicks

Fri 7th} chest and triceps at home

Tue 11th} arms workout

Wed 12th} 82 press-ups in one go

Thu 13th} chest and triceps workout plus a 2 mile jog

Tue 18th} 80 press-ups in one go

Wed 19th} stretching

Sat 22nd} chest and triceps plus 2 mile jog

Mon 24th} 100 pull-ups

Tue 25th} 60 press-ups

Wed 26th} 100 pull-ups (with weights)

Sun 30th} stretching and kicks

MAY 95

Mon 1st} 100 pull-ups (65 with weights)

Thu 4th} arms workout

Fri 5th} 2 mile jog

Sat 6th} 70 press-ups

Mon 8th} 102 pull-ups (77 with weights)

Tue 9th} chest and triceps workout

Thu 11th} arms workout

Mon 15th} 100 pull-ups (with weights)

Thu 18th} chest and triceps workout

Sun 21st} 150 squats with 11 stone

Mon 22nd} 101 pull-ups (76 with weights)

Tue 23rd} went to bodyworks gym

Sat 27th} 2 mile jog

Sun 28th} 70 press-ups

Mon 29th} 150 squats with 12 stone

Tue 30th} chest workout also some stretching

JUNE 95

Fri 2nd} arms workout

Wed 7th} 100 press-ups

Thu 8th} chest and triceps workout

Fri 9th} went to bodyworks gym

Tue 13th} went to bodyworks gym

Thu 15th} arms workout plus some stretching

Fri 16th} went to bodyworks gym

Mon 19th} my 25th birthday

Tue 20th} went to bodyworks gym plus 3 laps of the track

Thu 22nd} chest and arms workout

Fri 23rd} went to bodyworks gym plus 4 laps of the track

Sat 24th} 80 press-ups

Mon 26th} 100 pull-ups (75 with weights)

Tue 27th} went to bodyworks gym plus 5 laps of the track

Thu 29th} arms workout plus some stretching

Fri 30th} went to bodyworks gym

JULY 95

Tue 4th} arms workout plus some stretching

Fri 7th} 100 squats with 11 stone

Sat 8th} 130 press-ups (80,50)

Mon 10th} went to bodyworks gym

Wed 12th} went to bodyworks gym

Sun 16th} 120 press-ups (70,50)

Mon 17th} went to bodyworks gym plus 78 pull-ups (with weights)

Wed 19th} went to bodyworks gym

Fri 21st} went to bodyworks gym plus (88kg bench pressing at home)

Tue 25th} went to bodyworks gym

Wed 26th} 200 press-ups (70,50,40,40)

Fri 28th} went to bodyworks gym

Mon 31st} went to bodyworks gym plus some stretching

AUG 95

Tue 1st} went to bodyworks gym

Fri 4th} went to bodyworks gym

Mon 14th} went to bodyworks gym

Thu 17th} went to bodyworks gym

Tue 22nd} went to bodyworks gym

Wed 23rd} chest and triceps workout at home

Mon 28th} went to bodyworks gym

Thu 31st} went to bodyworks gym

SEPT 95

Fri 1st} 80 press-ups

Mon 4th} went to bodyworks gym plus stretching at home

Wed 6th} 80 press-ups

Fri 8th} went to bodyworks gym

Mon 11th} went to bodyworks gym plus arms end stretching at home

Wed 13th} went to bodyworks gym

Fri 15th} went to bodyworks gym

Mon 18th} Bench-pressing at home

Tue 19th} went to bodyworks gym

Wed 20th} 80 press-ups

Thu 21st} went to bodyworks gym

Mon 25th} 70 press-ups plus stretching at home

Tue 26th} went to bodyworks plus 80 press-ups

Thu 28th} went to bodyworks gym

Sat 30th} went to bodyworks gym

OCT 95

Mon 2nd} 85 press-ups

Tue 3rd} went to bodyworks gym

Fri 6th} went to bodyworks gym

Sat 7th} went to bodyworks gym

Tue 10th} went to bodyworks gym

Fri 13th} went to bodyworks gym

Sat 14th} 80 press-ups

Mon 16th} 102 pull-ups (60 with weights)

Tue 17th} went to bodyworks gym

Thu 19th} 80 press-ups

Fri 20th} went to bodyworks gym

Mon 23rd} 106 pull-ups (86 with weights)

Tue 24th} went to bodyworks gym

Fri 27th} went to bodyworks gym

NOV 95

Wed 1st} went to bodyworks gym

Thu 2nd} went to body works gym

Fri 3rd} 90 press-ups

Mon 6th} stretching at home

Tue 7th} went to bodyworks gym

Sat 11th} went to bodyworks gym

Mon 13th} stretching plus triceps at home

Tue 14th} went to bodyworks gym

Thu 16th} 80 press-ups

Fri 17th} went to bodyworks gym

Sat 18th} 60 press-ups

Tue 21st} went to bodyworks gym

Fri 24th} went to bodyworks gym

Sun 26th} 43 pull-ups in 2 goes

Mon 27th} chest and triceps at home

Tue 28th} went to bodyworks gym

DEC 95

Fri 1st} went to bodyworks gym

Tue 5th} went to bodyworks gym

Thu 7th} 140 press-ups plus some stretching

Fri 8th} went to bodyworks gym

Tue 12th} went to bodyworks gym

Thu 14th} 140 press-ups (80 then 60)

Mon 18th} went to bodyworks gym

Tue 19th} went to bodyworks gym

Fri 22nd} went to bodyworks gym

Tue 26th} 100 press-ups

Sat 30th} chest and triceps work out at home

1996

JAN 96

Tue 2nd} went to bodyworks gym

Fri 5th} went to bodyworks gym

Sat 6th} 70 press-ups

Tue 9th} went to bodyworks gym plus 130 press-ups (60,30,40)

Thu 11th} stretching plus a little arms workout

Fri 12th} went to bodyworks gym

Mon 15th} 80 press-ups

Tue 16th} went to bodyworks gym

Fri 19th} went to bodyworks gym

Mon 22nd} 110 pull-ups (75 with weights) plus 50 press-ups

Tue 23rd} went to bodyworks gym

Fri 26th} went to bodyworks gym

Tue 30th} went to bodyworks gym

FEB 96

Fri 2nd} went to bodyworks gym

Sat 3rd} 70 press-ups

Mon 5th} 100 pull-ups (78 with weights)

Tue 6th} went to bodyworks gym

Wed 7th} 30 press-ups plus an arms and stretching workout

Fri 9th} went to bodyworks gym

Tue 13th} went to bodyworks gym

Wed 14th} 80 press-ups

Fri 16th} went to bodyworks gym

Tue 20th} went to bodyworks gym

Fri 23rd} went to bodyworks gym

Mon 26th} chest, biceps and triceps workout at home on the bench

Tue 27th} went to bodyworks gym

MARCH 96

Fri 1st} went to bodyworks gym

Sat 2nd} went to bodyworks gym

Mon 4th} 60 press-ups

Tue 5th} went to bodyworks gym

Thu 7th} went to 5 a side football with work

Fri 8th} went to bodyworks gym

Mon 11th} 104 pull-ups (74 with weights)

Tue 12th} went to 5 aside football with work

Fri 15th} went to bodyworks gym

Mon 18th} 80 press-ups

Tue 19th} went to bodyworks gym plus 5 a side football with work

Fri 22nd} went to bodyworks gym

Mon 25th} 100 pull-ups (70 with weights)

Tue 26th} went to bodyworks gym plus 5 a side football with work

Fri 29th} went to bodyworks gym

APRIL 96

Tue 2nd} went to bodyworks gym plus a little arms workout at home

Fri 5th} went to bodyworks gym plus went swimming

Sat 6th} went swimming

Mon 8th} went to bodyworks gym

Tue 9th} 5 a side football with work

Fri 12th} went to bodyworks gym

Mon 15th} 100 pull-ups (80 with weights) plus arms workout

Tue 16th} went to bodyworks gym plus 5 a side football with work

Thu 18th} 50 press-ups

Fri 19th} went to bodyworks gym

Mon 22nd} 100 pull-ups (80 with weights)

Tue 23rd} went to bodyworks gym

Fri 26th} went to bodyworks gym

Tue 30th} went to bodyworks gym plus 5 a side football with work

May 96

Thu 2nd} 105 press-ups

Fri 3rd} went to bodyworks gym

Tue 7th} 5 a side football with work

Wed 8th} went to bodyworks gym

Fri 10th} went to bodyworks gym

Mon 13th} stretching exercises plus100 press-ups

Tue 14th} went to bodyworks gym

Fri 17th} went to bodyworks gym

Mon 20th} chest and triceps workout at home

Tue 21st} went to bodyworks gym

Fri 24th} went to bodyworks gym

JUNE 96

Mon 3rd} went to bodyworks gym

Tue 4th} 5 a side football with work

Fri 7th} went to bodyworks gym

Mon 10th} went to bodyworks gym plus 100 pull-ups

Tue 11th} 5 a side football with work

Fri 14th} went to bodyworks gym

Mon 17th} went to bodyworks gym plus 5 laps of the track and went mountain biking

Tue 18th} 5 a side football with work

Fri 21st} went to bodyworks gym

Mon 24th} went to bodyworks gym plus went mountain biking

Tue 25th} 5 a side football with work

Fri 28th} went to bodyworks gym

JULY 96

Mon 1st} went to bodyworks gym

Tue 2nd} 5 a side football with work

Fri 5th} went to bodyworks gym

Sat 6th} 80 press-ups (50,30)

Mon 8th} went to bodyworks gym

Tue 9th} 5 a side football with work

Fri 12th} went to bodyworks gym

Mon 15th} went to bodyworks gym

Tue 16th} 5 a side football with work

Fri 19th} went to bodyworks gym

Sat 20th} went swimming

Sun 21st} 70 press-ups

Mon 22nd} went to bodyworks gym

Tue 23rd} 5 a side football with work

Fri 26th} went to bodyworks gym

Mon 29th} went to bodyworks gym plus mountain biking and 60 press-ups

Tue 30th} 5 a side football with work

AUG 96

Fri 2nd} went to bodyworks gym

Mon 5th} went to bodyworks gym

Tue 6th} 35 press-ups plus arms workout and stretching at home

Fri 9th} went to bodyworks gym

Mon 12th} went to bodyworks gym plus mountain biking and arms workout

Fri 16th} went to bodyworks gym

Mon 19th} 60 press-ups plus arms and stretching at home

Fri 23rd} went to bodyworks gym

Mon 26th} went to bodyworks gym

Tue 27th} 60 press-ups plus some stretching

Fri 30th} went to bodyworks gym

SEP 96

Thu 5th} 60 press-ups

Sat 7th} 50 press-ups

Mon 9th} went to body works gym

Fri 13th} went to bodyworks gym

Mon 16th} went to bodyworks gym plus 60 press-ups

Fri 20th} went to bodyworks gym

Sun 22nd} arms workout at home

Mon 23rd} chest and triceps workout at home

Thu 26th} arms workout plus 50 press-ups

Mon 30th} chest and triceps at home plus 60 pull-ups (45 with weights)

OCT 96

Wed 2nd} 60 press-ups plus a little bit of stretching

Fri 4th} went to bodyworks gym

Mon 7th} 100 pull-ups (80 with weights) plus a little bit of stretching

Fri 11th} went to bodyworks gym

Mon 14th} 100 pull-ups (50 with weights) plus stretching chest and triceps workout

Fri 18th} went to bodyworks gym

Mon 21st} chest and triceps workout

Wed 23rd} 50 press-ups

Fri 25th} went to bodyworks gym

Mon 28th} chest and triceps workout pus some stretching and kicks

NOV 96

Fri 1st} went to bodyworks gym

Mon 4th} 100 pull-ups (80 with weights) plus went kickboxing for the first time

Fri 8th} went to bodyworks gym

Mon 11th} went kickboxing

Fri 15th} went to bodyworks gym

Mon 18th} went kickboxing plus arms workout and 100 press-ups (50,20,20,10)

Fri 22nd} went to bodyworks gym

Mon 25th} went kickboxing plus arms workout and stretching

Fri 29th} went to bodyworks gym

DEC 96

Mon 2nd} went kickboxing plus arms workout and some stretching

Fri 6th} went to bodyworks gym

Sun 8th} went kickboxing plus had a grading for yellow belt

Mon 9th} went kickboxing

Fri 13th} went to bodyworks gym

Sun 15th} 65 press ups in one go plus some stretching and kicks

Mon 16th} went kickboxing

Fri 20th} went to bodyworks gym

Sun 22nd} done some stretching and kicks

Mon 23rd} went kickboxing

Sat 28th} went to bodyworks gym

Mon 30th} went to a different gym body zone

1997

JAN 97

Fri 3rd} went to bodyworks gym

Mon 6th} went kickboxing plus arms workout

Fri 10th} went to bodyworks gym

Mon 13th} went kickboxing

Fri 17th} went to bodyworks gym

Sun 19th} 50 press-ups plus some stretching

Mon 20th} went kickboxing plus arms workout and stretching

Fri 24th} went to bodyworks gym

Mon 27th} went kickboxing plus arms workout

Fri 31st} went to bodyworks gym

FEB 97

Mon 10th} went kickboxing

Fri 14th} went to bodyworks gym

Mon 17th} went kickboxing plus arms workout

Sun 23rd} arms workout (200 arm curls on each arm with 10kg)

Mon 24th} went to body works gym

Thu 27th} 60 press-ups

Fri 28th} went to bodyworks gym

MARCH 97

Mon 3rd} went kickboxing

Fri 7th} went to bodyworks gym

Mon 10th} arms workout plus100 pull-ups (80 with weights)
Sun 16th} 40 press-ups

Mon 17th} went kickboxing plus arms workout

Sat 22nd} 60 press-ups

Mon 24th} went kickboxing plus 50 pull-ups (30 with weights)

Tue 25th} went to bodyworks gym

Fri 28th} went to bodyworks gym

APRIL 97

Thu 3rd} 60 press-ups plus stretching and kicks

Mon 7th} went to kickboxing plus 100 pull-ups (80 with weights)

Sat 12th} went to bodyworks gym

Tue 22nd} went to body works gym

Sat 26th} 60 press-ups

Mon 28th} went kickboxing

Wed 30th} went to bodyworks gym

MAY 97

Sat 3rd} 60 press-ups

Mon 5th} done kickboxing at home

Thu 8th} went to bodyworks gym

Mon 12th} went kickboxing

Thu 15th} went to bodyworks gym

Sun 18th} 70 press-ups

Tue 20th} went to body works gym

Fri 23rd} went to bodyworks gym

Wed 28th} 70 press-ups

Fri 30th} went to bodyworks gym

JUNE 97

Tue 3rd} went to bodyworks gym

Wed 4th} 60 press-ups

Sun 8th} kickboxing grading 3hrs: (got blue belt)

Mon 9th} went kickboxing

Wed 11th} went to bodyworks gym

Tue 17th} 70 press-ups

Wed 18th} went to bodyworks gym

Wed 25th} went to bodyworks gym

Mon 30th} went kickboxing

JULY 97

Wed 2nd} went to bodyworks gym

Thu 3rd} 70 press-ups

Mon 14th} went to bodyworks gym

Mon 21st} 11 a side football for work

Tue 22nd} arms workout plus some stretching

Fri 25th} went to bodyworks gym

Wed 30th} went to bodyworks gym

AUG 97

Thu 7th} went to bodyworks gym

Fri 8th} 70 press-ups plus some stretching

Tue 19th} went to bodyworks gym

Thu 28th} went to bodyworks gym

SEP 97

Mon 1st} 70 press-ups

Fri 5th} 60 press-ups

Sat 6th} arms workout plus went for a jog

Fri 12th} went to bodyworks gym

Mon 15th} arms workout plus some stretching

Fri 19th} went to bodyworks gym

Sun 21st} kickboxing at home plus some stretching

Fri 26th} went to bodyworks gym

OCT 97

Fri 3rd} went to bodyworks gym

Fri 10th} went to bodyworks gym

Fri 17th} went to bodyworks gym

Mon 27th} went to bodyworks gym

Fri 31st} went to bodyworks gym

NOV 97

Fri 7th} went to bodyworks gym

Fri 14th} went to bodyworks gym

Sun 16th} kickboxing at home

Fri 21st} went to bodyworks gym

Thu 27th} went to bodyworks gym

DEC 97

Mon 1st} stretching at home

Fri 5th} went to bodyworks gym

Thu 11th} went to bodyworks gym

Thu 18th} went to bodyworks gym

Tue 23rd} kickboxing at home plus some stretching

Sun 28th} 6-mile jog

Mon 29th} chest and triceps workout at home

Wed 31st} went to bodyworks gym

1998

JAN 98

Sun 4th} 70 press-ups plus a little arms workout

Thu 8th} went to bodyworks gym

Tue 13th} 75 press-ups

Thu 15th} went to bodyworks gym

Thu 22nd} went to bodyworks gym

Mon 26th} 60 press-ups plus some stretching

Thu 29th} went to bodyworks gym

FEB 98

Thu 5th} went to bodyworks gym

Mon 9th} done some kickboxing

Thu 12th} went to bodyworks gym

Fri 20th} went to bodyworks gym

Thu 26th} went to bodyworks gym plus 60 press-ups

MARCH 98

Wed 4th} went to Virginia Waters and done 6-mile jog

Thu 5th} stretching and stomach workout

Sun 8th} 60 press-ups plus arms workout

Thu 12th} went to bodyworks gym

Fri 13th} 60 press-ups

Thu 19th} went to bodyworks gym

Thu 26th} 102 pull-ups (82 with weights) plus 50 press-ups and some stretching

APRIL 98

Thu 2nd} went to bodyworks gym

Wed 8th} went to bodyworks gym plus 15 mins: on the punch bag

Tue 14th} 101 pull-ups (81 with weights)

Thu 16th} went to bodyworks gym

Thu 23rd} went to bodyworks gym plus 20 mins: on the bag

Mon 27th} 10 mins: on the bag

Thu 30th} went to bodyworks gym

MAY 98

Sun 3rd} 60 press-ups plus some leg stretches

Thu 7th} went to bodyworks gym

Mon 11th} 40 press-ups plus 15 mins: on the bag and 5 mins: skipping

Thu 14th} went to bodyworks gym plus 5 mins: on the bag

Sun 17th} stomach and arms workout

Mon 18th} 5-mile jog

Thu 21st} went to bodyworks gym plus 2.5-mile jog

Tue 26th} 5-mile jog plus 15 mins: on the bag

Thu 28th} went to bodyworks gym

JUNE 98

Mon 1st} 4-mile jog (time: *28.56.81*)

Thu 4th} 2-mile jog (time: *14.28.52*) plus 30 mins: on the bag

Sun 7th} 10k road race at Spelthorne in Staines

Thu 11th} went to bodyworks gym plus 25 mins: on the bag

Mon 15th} 2-mile jog (time: *13.49.97*) plus 25 mins: on the bag

Thu 18th} 2-mile jog (time: *14.02.74*) plus 20 mins: on the bag also arms workout

Tue 23rd} 50 press-ups

Thu 25th} went to bodyworks gym plus 20 mins: on the bag

Mon 29th} 25 mins: on the bag plus arms and stomach workout

JULY 98

Thu 2nd} went to bodyworks gym plus 20 mins: on the bag

Mon 6th} 25 mins: on the bag

Thu 9th} went to bodyworks gym

Sun 12th} arms workout 200 reps with 12kg

Mon 13th} 30 mins: on the bag

Thu 16th} 4-mile jog plus went mountain biking and 50 press-ups and arms workout

Tue 21st} 2-mile jog (time: *13.52.65*) plus 20 mins: on the bag

Thu 23rd} went to bodyworks gym

Mon 27th} 2-mile jog (time: *14.12.80*) plus 20 mins: on the bag

Thu 30th} went to bodyworks gym

AUG 98

Tue 4th} 2-mile jog time (time: *13.56.62*) plus 30 mins: on the bag

Thu 6th} went to bodyworks gym

Sun 9th} arms workout 200 reps with 12kg plus 90 press-ups (60,30)

Mon 10th} 4-mile jog, 2-miles in (time: *14.22.30*)

Thu 13th} went to bodyworks gym plus 20 mins: on the bag

Sun 16th} arms workout 200 reps with 12kg plus some stretching

Mon 17th} 2-mile jog (time: *14.13.71*) plus 15 mins: on the bag

Thu 20th} 2-mile jog (time: *13.52.04*) plus 100 pull-ups

Thu 27th} went to bodyworks gym plus 20 mins: on the bag

Mon 31st} arms workout 200 reps with 12kg

SEP 98

Tue 1st} 2-mile jog (time: *13.27.71*) plus 20 mins: on the bag and 100 pull-ups

Thu 3rd} arms workout plus some stretching

Sun 6th} arms workout 50 reps on each arm with 20kg

Mon 7th} 4-mile jog, 2-miles in (time: *13.21.13*) plus 20 mins: on the bag

Thu 10th} went to bodyworks gym

Mon 14th} on the bag for 25 mins:

Thu 17th} 2-mile jog (time: *12.59.11*), arms workout, 70 pull-ups and 40 press-ups

Mon 21st} 2-mile jog (time: *12.54.32*) plus 20 mins: on the bag and 60 press-ups

Thu 24th} went to bodyworks gym

Mon 28th} 2-mile jog (time: *12.51.25*) plus 25 mins: on the bag

OCT 98

Thu 1st} 4-mile jog (time: *28.30.32*) plus arms, stretching and stomach workout

Mon 5th} 25 mins: on the bag plus some stretching

Fri 9th} went to bodyworks gym

Sun 11th} went swimming

Mon 12th} 4-mile jog, 2-mile (time: *13.38.06*) 4-mile (time: *28.30.87*)

Tue 13th} 25 mins: on the bag

Thu 15th} 4-mile jog, 2-mile (time: *13.47.44*) 4-mile (time: *28.52.70*)

Sun 18th} 10-mile jog at Virginia Waters

Mon 19th} 30 mins: on the bag plus arms workout

Wed 21st} arms workout 200 reps on each arm with 8kg, done in 10's

Thu 22nd} went to bodyworks gym

Sun 25th} 5-mile jog at Virginia Waters

Thu 29th} 40 mins jog, 2-miles in (time: *13.31.58*) plus arms, stretching and bag

NOV 98

Sun 1st} 10-mile jog at Virginia Waters

Mon 2nd} 100 pull-ups

Thu 5th} went to bodyworks gym

Sun 8th} 10-mile jog at Virginia Waters

Mon 9th} went on the bag for 25 mins:

Thu 12th} arms workout plus 40 press-ups on supports

Sun 15th} 10-mile jog at Virginia Waters

Mon 16th} 110 pull-ups (55 with weights) plus some stomach workout

Thu 19th} went to bodyworks gym

Mon 23rd} 100 pull-ups (58 with weights)

Thu 26th} went to bodyworks gym

DEC 98

Thu 3rd} went to bodyworks gym

Fri 4th} went on the bag for 20 mins:

Thu 10th} arms workout plus some kickboxing

Mon 14th} arms workout plus some stretching and stomach exercises

Thu 17th} went to bodyworks gym plus some skipping

Mon 21st} went to bodyworks gym

Sun 27th} went on the bag for 30 mins: plus went mountain biking

Wed 30th} went to bodyworks gym

1999

JAN 99

Fri 1st} arms workout 100 reps on each arm with 8kg

Mon 4th} 100 pull-ups

Thu 7th} arms workout plus some stretching and skipping

Mon 11th} 100 pull-ups (70 with weights)

Thu 14th} went to bodyworks gym

Sat 16th} went on the bag for 15 mins:

Wed 20th} 100 pull-ups plus some stretching

Thu 21st} arms workout

Sun 24th} went to bodyworks gym

Thu 28th} 100 pull-ups (80 with leg weights)

Sat 30th} went on the bag for 30 mins:

FEB 99

Mon 1st} 50 press-ups on stands

Thu 4th} went to bodyworks gym plus 50 press-ups on stands

Mon 8th} 100 pull-ups

Thu 11th} went to bodyworks gym

Mon 15th} 100 pull-ups (80 with leg weights)

Thu 18th} went to bodyworks gym

Thu 25th} went to bodyworks gym

Sun 28th} arms workout 200 reps on each arm with 8kg

MARCH 99

Thu 4th} went to bodyworks gym

Fri 5th} went on the bag for 30 mins:

Thu 11th} went to bodyworks gym

Sun 14th} went on the bag for 30 mins:

Thu 16th} 60 press-ups

Thu 18th} went to bodyworks gym

Thu 25th} went to bodyworks gym

Sun 28th} 104 pull-ups

Mon 29th} went on the bag for 40 mins:

APRIL 99

Thu 1st} went to bodyworks gym

Mon 5th} played golf plus done 104 pull-ups

Thu 8th} went to bodyworks gym

Fri 9th} played golf

Sat 10th} played golf

Mon 12th} went on the bag for 30 mins: plus 50 pull-ups

Thu 15th} arms workout plus some stomach and stretching

Sat 18th} 103 pull-ups (83 with 2.5kg weights) plus went swimming

Mon 19th} 2-mile jog (time 13.59.03) plus 20 mins: on the bag

Thu 22nd} went to bodyworks gym

Sun 25th} went swimming

Mon 26th} 2-mile jog (time 13.50.37) plus 15 mins: on the bag

Thu 29th} went to bodyworks gym plus 15 mins: on the bag

MAY 99

Sat 1st} played golf

Mon 3rd} arms workout 100 reps on each arm with 8kg

Tue 4th} 2.5-mile jog 2-miles in (time 13.25.60)

Thu 6th} went to bodyworks gym

Fri 7th} went on the bag for 20 mins:

Mon 10th} 2.5-mile jog 2-miles in (time 13.29.46)

Wed 12th} 50 press-ups

Thu 13th} went to bodyworks gym

Sun 16th} 60 press-ups plus arms workout

Tue 18th} 31 mins jog 2-miles in (time 13.30.10) plus 25 mins: on the bag

Thu 20th} went to bodyworks gym

Tue 25th} arms workout with a range of weights from 2kg to 20kg

Wed 26th} 43 mins jog 2-miles in (time 13.38.27) plus 20 mins: on the bag

Mon 31st} 100 pull-ups (80 with 4.5kg weight) plus arms, stretching and stomach

JUNE 99

Tue 1st} 45 mins jog 2-miles in (time 13.39.67) plus 20 mins: on the bag

Thu 3rd} went to bodyworks gym

Tue 8th} 30 mins jog

Thu 10th} went to bodyworks gym

Sun 13th} ran in Spelthorne 10k road race

Mon 14th} 25 mins: on the bag

Thu 17th} went to bodyworks gym

Mon 21st} 25 mins: on the bag

Thu 24th} went to bodyworks gym

Sun 27th} 100 pull-ups (80 with weights)

JULY 99

Thu 1st} went to bodyworks gym plus 25mins: on the bag

Mon 5th} 19 mins jog 2-miles in (time 13.47.50)

Thu 8th} went to bodyworks gym

Sun 11th} 70 press-ups

Mon 12th} 21 min jog 2-miles in (time 13.39.57) plus 15mins: on the bag

Tue 13th} 100 pull-ups

Sat 17th} 100 pull-ups plus 100 reps on each arm with 8kg

Mon 19th} 28 min jog 2-miles in (time 13.57.24) plus 20 mins: on the bag

Sun 25th} 60 press-ups

Mon 26th} 32 min jog 2-miles in (time 13.10.25) plus 20 mins: on the bag

Thu 29th} went to bodyworks gym

Sat 31st} 100 pull-ups

AUG 99

Sun 1st} 60 press-ups

Mon 2nd} 28 min jog plus 20 mins: on the bag

Thu 5th} went to bodyworks gym

Sun 8th} arms workout 100 reps with 8gk on each arm plus 70 press-ups

Mon 9th} 40 min jog 2-miles in (time 13.34.67)

Thu 12th} went to bodyworks gym

Fri 13th} played baseball with work

Mon 16th} 31 min jog plus 25 mins: on the bag

Thu 19th} 2-mile jog in (time 13.06.11) plus 100 pull-ups (80 w/w) and 60 press-ups

Mon 23rd} 60 press-ups

Thu 26th} went to bodyworks gym

Fri 27th} 20 mins: on the bag

Sun 29th} ran in Pewsey Vale 5 mile road race (time 37.31.24)

SEPT 99

Wed 1st} 60 press-ups

Thu 2nd} 2-mile jog in (time 13.13.37) plus 100 pull-ups (70 with weights)

Sun 5th} stomach workout

Mon 6th} 2 lots of 40 press-ups on stands plus 25 mins: on the bag and arms workout

Thu 9th} went to bodyworks gym

Thu 16th} went to bodyworks gym

Tue 21st} 100 pull-ups (80 with weights)

Wed 22nd} 60 press-ups

Thu 23rd} went to bodyworks gym plus 20 mins: on the bag

Thu 30th} 19 min jog plus 30 mins: on the bag and 35 press-ups on stands

OCT 99

Sun 3rd} 50 press-ups

Tue 5th} went to bodyworks gym plus 19 min jog 2-miles in (time 13 48.40)

Fri 8th} 25 mins: on the bag

Sun 10th} 19 min jog 2-miles in (time 14.13.65)

Tue 12th} 100 pull-ups (70 with weights)

Thu 14th} arms workout plus 2 lots of 40 press-ups on stands and stomach workout

Thu 21st} went to bodyworks gym

Mon 25th} 100 press-ups 60,40

Thu 28th} 30 mins: on the bag plus 100 pull-ups (75 w/w) and 60 press-ups on stands

Sun 31st} 18 min jog

NOV 99

Tue 2nd} 40 press-ups

Thu 4th} went to bodyworks gym

Wed 10th} 127 pull-ups (123 with weights)

Thu 11th} 20 mins: on the bag

Thu 18th} went to bodyworks gym

Thu 25th} went to bodyworks gym

Tue 30th} 136 pull-ups (110 with weights)

DEC 99

Thu 2nd} went to bodyworks gym

Sun 5th} 20 min jog 2-miles in (time 14.09.21)

Tue 7th} 111 pull-ups (80 with weights)

Thu 9th} went to bodyworks gym

Wed 15th} 25 mins: on the bag

Thu 16th} went to bodyworks gym

Thu 23rd} went to bodyworks gym

Tue 28th} 20 min jog 2-miles in (time 14.25.23) plus 30 mins: on the bag

Fri 31st} 139 pull-ups (100 with weights)

2000

JAN 2000

Sun 2nd} 60 press-ups

Sun 8th} 50 press-ups plus 100 curls on each arm with 8kg

Thu 13th} went to bodyworks gym

Sun 16th} 5.5-mile jog over Virginia Waters

Mon 17th} 50 press-ups

Tue 18th} 50 press-ups

Thu 20th} 150 pull-ups (113 with weights)

Sat 22nd} went on the bag for 40 min's

Thu 27th} went to bodyworks gym

Sun 30th} 10-mile jog over Virginia Waters

FEB 2000

Thu 3rd} arms workout plus 50 pull-ups

Sun 6th} 150 pull-ups (89 with weights)

Thu 10th} went to bodyworks gym

Fri 25th} 150 pull-ups (92 with weights) plus 40 press-ups

Sun 27th} 100 arm curls on each arm with 8kg

MARCH 2000

Thu 2nd} went to bodyworks gym

Wed 8th} 30: mins on the bag

Fri 10th} 50 press-ups plus 70 leg raises on pull-up bar and 100 curls with 8kg

Mon 13th} went to bodyworks gym

Thu 23rd} 120 pull-ups (75 with weights) plus some arm curls

Wed 29th} went to bodyworks gym

APRIL 2000

Sun 2nd} went on the bag for 20: min's

Wed 5th} 133 pull-ups (93 with weights)

Wed 12th} went to bodyworks gym

Sun 16th} 16-min jog plus 20 min's on the bag

Wed 19th} 72 pull-ups (44 with weights)

Thu 20th} 100 arm curls on each arm with 12kg plus some stomach exercises

Sun 23rd} 120 arm curls plus 105 press-ups (55,50)

Sat 29th} went to bodyworks gym

Sun 30th} went for a jog plus 15 min's on the bag

MAY 2000

Mon 1st} 100 arm curls on each arm with 12kg

Thu 4th} 50 press-ups

Sat 6th} 25 pull-ups

Sun 7th} 14 min jog

Wed 10th} 22 min jog, 101 pull-ups (71 with weights), 30 press-ups and stomach

Thu 11th} 50 arm curls on each arm with 12kg

Fri 12th} 50 press-ups

Sun 14th} 25 min's on the bag plus 21 min jog 2-mile's in (14.23 67)

Tue 16th} 103 pull-ups (88 with weights) plus105 press-ups and 100 curls with 12kg

Sun 21st} 35 min jog

Wed 24th} went to bodyworks gym

Thu 25th} 150 press-ups (50,50,50)

Fri 26th} 50 press-ups

Sat 27th} little arms and stomach workout

Sun 28th} 24 min jog

Mon 29th} 5.5-mile jog over Virginia Waters

JUNE 2000

Thu 1st} 23 min jog plus 50 press-ups

Fri 2nd} 30 leg raises

Sun 4th} 41 min jog plus 100 curls on each arm with 12kg

Tue 6th} went to bodyworks gym

Thu 8th} 35 min jog

Sat 10th} 20 min's on the bag

Sun 11th} 7-mile jog over Virginia Waters

Wed 14th} went to bodyworks gym

Thu 15th} 15 min jog

Sun 18th} 10k road race at Spelthorne near Staines (time 49.41.02)

Mon 19th} 90 press-ups (40,50) plus 51 pull-ups (36 w/w) and 100 curls with 12kg

Sat 24th} 111 leg raises plus130 arm curls with 16kg and 20 mins on the bag

Mon 26th} 2-mile jog plus 102 arm curls with 12kg, 69 pull-ups and 120 press-ups

JULY 2000

Sat 1st} 50 press-ups

Mon 3rd} 2-mile jog plus 101 pull-ups (66 with 12kg weight), 160 press-ups, 100 curls

Wed 5th} went to bodyworks gym

Tue 11th} went to bodyworks gym

Thu 13th} 2-mile jog

Fri 14th} 100 press-ups

Sun 16th} 15 min's on the bag

Mon 17th} went to bodyworks gym

Sat 22nd} 2-mile jog

Sun 23rd} 101 pull-ups (66 with weights) plus 100 arm curls with 12kg

Tue 25th} 210 press-ups (30,30,30,20,30,30,20,20) plus 90 leg raises

Thu 27th} 80 press-ups (30,50) plus some various arms workout

AUG 2000

Tue 1st} went to bodyworks gym

Thu 3rd} 2-mile jog

Sat 5th} 50 press-ups

Tue 8th} went to bodyworks gym

Wed 9th} 2-mile jog

Sat 13th} 300 press-ups

Wed 16th} went to bodyworks gym

Sun 20th} 19 min jog 2-miles in (time 13.56.01) plus 25 min's on the bag

Wed 23rd} went to bodyworks gym

Mon 28th} 15 min jog plus 300 press-ups

SEPT 2000

Mon 4th} 315 press-ups

Wed 6th} went to bodyworks gym

Sat 9th} leg raises plus a little arms workout

Sun 10th} 15 min jog

Thu 21st} 320 press-ups plus 20 mins on the bag

Sun 24th} 325 press-ups

Tue 26th} 100 arm curls plus some stretching

OCT 2000

Sun 1st} 15 min run

Tue 3rd} went to bodyworks gym

Wed 4th} 100 pull-ups (70 with weights)

Sat 7th} 120 arm curls plus some leg raises

Sun 8th} 28k walk for charity (motor neuron disease)

Fri 13th} 15 min's on the bag

Sat 14th} 18 min jog

Wed 18th} 27 min jog

Sun 22nd} 27 min jog

Wed 25th} went to bodyworks gym

Sun 29th} 38 min jog

Tue 31st} went to bodyworks gym

NOV 2000

Sun 5th} 27 min jog

Tue 7th} 270 press-ups on stands

Wed 8th} 16 min jog

Sat 11th} 38 min jog

Mon 13th} 16 min jog plus 300 press-ups

Tue 14th} went to bodyworks gym

Thu 16th} 310 press-ups in 10 goes

Fri 17th} 16 min jog

Sun 19th} 10k road race at Brighton in (time 47.32.29)

Mon 20th} went to bodyworks gym

Thu 23rd} 331 press-ups in 11 goes

Fri 24th} 17 min jog

Tue 28th} went to bodyworks gym

Thu 30th} 310 press-ups (30,40,40,30,40,20,30,30,25,25)

DEC 2000

Sun 3rd} 26 min jog

Wed 6th} went to bodyworks gym

Sun 10th} 20 min jog plus 105 arm curls and 25 min's on the bag

Mon 11th} went to bodyworks gym

Wed 13th} 320 press-ups (40,35,40,40,40,35,25,25,25,15)

Fri 15th} 16 min jog

Mon 18th} 100 pull-ups

Fri 22nd} went to bodyworks gym

Sun 24th} 27 min jog

Fri 29th} 16 min jog

2001

JAN 2001

Mon 1st} 25 min's on the bag plus 100 arm curls with 12kg

Wed 3rd} 55 pull-ups, 180 press-ups, 55 arm curls

Sun 7th} 7-mile jog at Virginia Waters

Wed 10th} went to bodyworks gym

Sun 14th} 17 min jog

Mon 15th} went to bodyworks gym

Fri 19th} 17 min jog

Sun 21st} 5.5-mile jog at Virginia Waters

Tue 23rd} 165 press-ups, 61 pull-ups, 56 arm curls on each arm with 12kg

Sun 28th} 40 min jog

Mon 29th} went to bodyworks gym plus 17 min jog

FEB 2001

Sun 4th} Chichester 10k road race, time in (47.58.02)

Wed 7th} went to bodyworks gym

Sun 11th} 25 min's on the bag

Thu 15th} went to bodyworks gym

Sun 18th} 15 min's on the bag

Wed 21st} went to bodyworks gym

MARCH 2001

Fri 2nd} went to bodyworks gym

Sat 3rd} 50 press-ups

Sun 4th} 15 min jog

Wed 7th} 50 press-ups

Thu 8th} went to bodyworks gym

Sat 10th} 50 leg raises

Sun 18th} 14 min jog

Thu 22nd} went to bodyworks gym

Thu 29th} 20 min's on the bag

Fri 30th} went to bodyworks gym

APRIL 2001

Thu 5th} went to bodyworks gym

Sat 7th} 20 min's on the bag

Tue 10th} 120 press-ups (30,30,40,20)

Fri 13th} went to bodyworks gym

Mon 16th} 13 min jog

Thu 19th} 155 press-ups plus 100 pull-ups

Wed 25th} 150 press-ups plus 100 pull-ups

Thu 26th} 26 min jog

Fri 27th} 110 arm curls on each arm with 12kg

MAY 2001

Tue 1st} went to bodyworks gym

Sun 6th} 20 min's on the bag plus 20 min jog

Tue 8th} 150 press-ups plus 100 pull-ups (30 with weights)

Mon 14th} 200 press-ups, 104 pull-ups plus 110 arm curls on each arm

Thu 17th} went to bodyworks gym

Sun 20th} 20 min's on the bag

Wed 23rd} 24 min jog

Fri 25th} 20 min's on the bag plus100 pull-ups and 205 press-ups (in 8 goes)

Mon 28th} 26 min jog

Thu 31st} went to bodyworks gym

JUNE 2001

Sun 3rd} 30 min jog plus went swimming

Mon 4th} went to bodyworks gym

Thu 7th} 30 min jog

Sat 9th} 200 press-ups (50,60,50,40)

Sun 10th} 26 min jog

Wed 13th} 33 min jog

Thu 14th} went to bodyworks gym

Sun 17th} Spelthorne 10k road race time in (46.50.12) plus 20 min's on the bag

Thu 21st} went to bodyworks gym

Mon 25th} 200 press-ups (40,50,50,30,30)

Tue 26th} 104 pull-ups (20,14,20,15,10,15,10)

Thu 28th} went to bodyworks gym

JULY 2001

Sun 1st} 3-mile jog

Sun 8th} 100arm curls on each arm with 14 kg plus stomach workout

Thu 12th} went to bodyworks gym

Sun 15th} 15 min's on the bag

Wed 18th} went to bodyworks gym

Sun 22nd} 13 min jog

Mon 23rd} 100 pull-ups (70 with weights) plus 200press-ups (50,60,35,50,5)

Wed 25th} went to bodyworks gym

Fri 27th} 12 min jog

Mon 30th} 12 min jog

AUG 2001

Wed 1st} went to bodyworks gym

Sat 4th} 12 min jog

Sun 5th} 20 min's on the bag

Tue 7th} 12 min jog

Thu 9th} went to bodyworks gym

Sun 12th} 12 min jog

Tue 14th} went to bodyworks gym

Sat 18th} 20 min jog, done 2 miles in time (12.33.02)

Tue 21st} 20 min jog, done 2-miles in time (13.01.04)

Thu 23rd} went to bodyworks gym

Tue 28th} 20 min jog, done 2-miles in time (13.21.86)

Thu 30th} 109 pull-ups, 200 press-ups plus 30 leg raises

SEPT 2001

Sun 2nd} 12 min jog

Wed 5th} 23 min jog

Sat 8th} 20 min's on the bag

Sun 9th} 26 min jog

Tue 11th} 23 min jog

Wed 12th} 210 press-ups, 100 pull-ups (25 with leg raises)

Sun 16th} 31 min jog plus 15 min's on the bag

Tue 18th} 12 min jog

Wed 19th} 101 pull-ups, 202 press-ups plus 50 sit-ups

Sun 23rd} 20 min jog, done 2-miles in time (13.09.69)

Wed 26th} 32 min jog

Thu 27th} went to bodyworks gym

Sat 29th} 41 min jog

OCT 2001

Tue 2nd} 39 min jog

Thu 4th} went to bodyworks gym

Sun 7th} 10k Sam Run at Wellington College in Crothorne time in (45.42.25)

Tue 9th} 12 min jog

Thu 11th} went to bodyworks gym

Sun 14th} 15 min's on the bag

Wed 17th} 12 min jog

Fri 19th} went to bodyworks gym

Sun 21st} 105 pull-ups (55 with leg weights)

Mon 22nd} 13 min jog

Thu 25th} went to bodyworks gym

Wed 31st} 100 arm curls on each arm with 14 kg

NOV 2001

Thu 1st} 210 press-ups (40,30,50,50,40)

Sat 3rd} 20 min's on the bag

Thu 8th} went to bodyworks gym

Thu 15th} went to bodyworks gym

Thu 22nd} went to bodyworks gym

Sun 25th} 15 min's on the bag

DEC 2001

Mon 3rd} 205 press-ups (165 with push-up stands 40,30,30,40,40,25)

Wed 5th} went to bodyworks gym

Wed 12th} 104 pull-ups (74 with leg weights)

Mon 17th} went to bodyworks gym

Thu 20th} 200 press-ups (35,40,40,40,40,5)

Thu 27th} went to bodyworks gym

Fri 28th} 13 min jog

2002

JAN 2002

Tue 1st} 13 min jog plus 205 press-ups (30,40,25,20,20,25,15,10,10,10)

Thu 3rd} went to bodyworks gym

Sun 6th} 12 min jog and 25 min's on the bag

Thu 10th} went to bodyworks gym

Sun 13th} 14 min jog

Thu 17th} went to bodyworks gym

Sun 20th} 15 min jog

Thu 24th} 14 min jog

Sat 26th} 23 min jog

Sun 27th} 13 min jog

Thu 31st} went to bodyworks gym

FEB 2002

Sat 2nd} 210 press-ups (30,30,40,35,30,30,15)

Sun 3rd} 16 min jog plus 20 min's on the bag

Thu 7th} went to bodyworks gym

Sun 10th} 16 min jog

Wed 13th} 15 min jog

Thu 14th} went to bodyworks gym

Sun 17th} 15 min jog

Tue 19th} 15 min jog

Thu 21st} went to bodyworks gym

Fri 22nd} 15 min jog

Sun 24th} 20 min's on the bag

Mon 25th} 16 min jog

MARCH 2002

Fri 1st} 15 min jog

Mon 4th} 23 min jog

Tue 5th} 100 pull-ups (12,15,15,10,16,10,12,10)

Thu 7th} went to bodyworks gym

Sun 10th} 23 min jog

Wed 13th} 23 min jog

Thu 14th} went to bodyworks gym

Sun 17th} 23 min jog

Thu 21st} went to bodyworks gym

Sat 23rd} 24 min jog

Mon 25th} 23 min jog

Thu 28th} went to bodyworks gym

Sat 30th} 23 min jog

APRIL 2002

Mon 1st} 22 min jog

Thu 4th} 22 min jog plus 201 press-ups (35,30,30,30,20,40,16)

Sat 6th} 28 min jog

Mon 8th} 22 min jog

Thu 11th} went to bodyworks gym

Sat 13th} 22 min jog

Mon 15th} 22 min jog

Wed 17th} went to bodyworks gym

Fri 19th} 22 min jog

Sun 21st} 28 min jog plus 20 min's on the bag

Tue 23rd} 22 min jog

Thu 25th} went to bodyworks gym

Sun 28th} 22 min jog

Tue 30th} 22 min jog

MAY 2002

Thu 2nd} went to bodyworks gym

Fri 3rd} 22 min jog

Mon 6th} 30 min jog

Thu 9th} went to bodyworks gym

Sat 11th} 38 min jog

Sun 12th} 20 min's on the bag

Mon 13th} 29 min jog

Thu 16th} 22 min jog

Fri 17th} 202 press-ups (30,40,30,30,20,20,17,15) plus some stomach exercises

Sun 19th} Bognor 10k road race time (45.49.70)

Wed 22nd} 22 min jog

Thu 23rd} went to bodyworks gym

Sun 26th} Spelthorne 10k road race time (44.11.10)

Thu 30th} went to bodyworks gym

Fri 31st} 22 min jog

JUNE 2002

Mon 3rd} 22 min jog

Wed 5th} 22 min jog

Thu 6th} went to bodyworks gym

Sun 9th} 37 min jog plus 20 min's on the bag

Wed 12th} 21 min jog

Thu 13th} went to bodyworks gym

Fri 14th} 23 min jog

Sun 16th} 38 min jog

Wed 19th} 22 min jog

Thu 20th} 104 pull-ups (65 with weights) 72 arm curls on each arm with 12kg

Sat 22nd} Datchet 10k road race time in (44.35.81)

Sun 23rd} jogged 5 laps of local track

Wed 26th} 22 min jog

Thu 27th} 205 press-ups (30,30,20,20,25,40,25,15)

Sat 29th} went to bodyworks gym

Sun 30th} 44 min jog

JULY 2002

Tue 2nd} 22 min jog

Thu 4th} 22 min jog

Sun 7th} Sam Run 10k race time in (44.31.21) came 48th

Thu 11th} went to bodyworks gym

Sun 14th} 20 min's on the bag

Thu 18th} went to bodyworks gym

Tue 23rd} 200 press-ups

Thu 25th} 15 min jog

Sat 27th} 106 pull-ups (10,20,15,10,10,11,12,10,8) plus 210 press-ups

Mon 29th} 23 min jog

Wed 31st} went to bodyworks gym

AUG 2002

Sun 4th} 22 min jog plus 20 min's on the bag

Thu 8th} went to bodyworks gym

Thu 15th} went to bodyworks gym

Thu 22nd} went to bodyworks gym

Mon 26th} 23 min jog

Thu 29th} went to bodyworks gym

SEP 2002

Sun 1st} 19 min jog plus 20 min's on the bag

Wed 4th} 23 min jog

Sun 8th} 22 min jog

Wed 11th} 22 min jog

Thu 12th} went to bodyworks gym

Sun 15th} 36 min jog

Tue 17th} 22 min jog

Thu 19th} 22 min jog

Sun 22nd} 43 min jog

Tue 24th} 22 min jog

Thu 26th} went to bodyworks gym

Sat 28th} 25 min's on the bag

Sun 29th} Camberley 10k road race time in (44.48.19)

OCT 2002

Fri 4th} 210 press-ups (30,20,40,30,20,30,20,20)

Mon 7th} went to bodyworks gym

Tue 15th} 23 min jog

Wed 16th} 101 pull-ups (71 with weights)

Mon 21st} went to bodyworks gym plus 20 min's on the bag

Mon 28th} went to bodyworks gym

NOV 2002

Thu 7th} 23 min jog

Mon 11th} went to bodyworks gym

Mon 18th} went to bodyworks gym plus 20 min's on the bag

Sun 24th} 200 press-ups (30,30,15,30,40,20,15,20)

Mon 25th} went to bodyworks gym

DEC 2002

Sun 1st} 23 min jog plus 205 press-ups and 67 leg raises on pull-up bar

Sun 8th} went to bodyworks gym

Mon 9th} 20 min's on the bag

Mon 16th} went to bodyworks gym

Mon 23rd} went to bodyworks gym

Sun 29th} 210 press-ups (30,30,30,40,40,20,10,10)

Mon 30th} went to bodyworks gym

2003

JAN 2003

Thu 9th} 240 press-ups on press-up stands (40,40,30,30,20,30,30,20)

Sun 12th} 20 min's on the bag

Mon 13th} went to bodyworks gym

Mon 20th} went to bodyworks gym

Sun 26th} 20 min's on the bag

Mon 27th} went to bodyworks gym

FEB 2003

Mon 3rd} went to bodyworks gym

Mon 10th} 3-mile jog time (22.45.55)

Fri 14th} 3-mile jog time (22.18.63)

Mon 17th} went to bodyworks gym

Tue 18th} 3-mile jog time (22.23.37)

Sun 23rd} 3-mile jog time (22.30.66

Mon 24th} went to bodyworks gym plus 20 min's on the bag

Wed 26th} 3-mile jog time (22.51.33)

MARCH 2008

Sat 1st} 3-mile jog time (22.11.12)

Tue 4th} 3-mile jog time (22.03.82)

Fri 7th} 3-mile jog time (21.28.59) plus 250 press-ups (30,30,30,40,30,20,20,20,30)

Mon 10th} went to bodyworks gym plus 30 min jog

Wed 12th} 28 min jog

Sat 15th} 26 min jog

Wed 19th} 36 min jog

Fri 21st} 3-mile jog time (22.05.31)

Sun 23rd} 25 min's on the bag

Mon 24th} went to bodyworks gym plus 44 min jog

Wed 26th} 27 min jog

Fri 28th} 105 pull-ups (68 with weights)

Sun 30th} Woking 10k road race time (46.16.19)

Mon 31st} went to bodyworks gym

APRIL 2003

Wed 2nd} 3-mile jog time (21.16.51)

Sun 6th} 28 min jog

Mon 7th} went to bodyworks gym

Wed 9th} 27 min jog

Sat 12th} 32 min jog

Mon 14th} went to bodyworks gym

Tue 15th} 31 min jog

Fri 18th} 31 min jog

Mon 21st} 28 min jog

Thu 24th} 31 min jog

Sun 27th} 34 min jog plus 20 min's on the bag

Mon 28th} went to bodyworks gym

Wed 30th} 32 min jog

MAY 2003

Fri 2nd} 3-mile jog time (20.57.14) a p.b.

Sun 4th} went swimming

Mon 5th} 30 min jog

Tue 6th} went to bodyworks gym

Thu 8th} 30 min jog

Fri 9th} 100 pull-ups (65 with weights) 25,10,10,10,17,10,8,10)

Mon 12th} 51 min jog

Thu 15th} 30 min jog

Sun 18th} 48 min jog

Mon 19th} went to bodyworks gym

Wed 21st} 30 min jog

Sun 25th} Spelthorne 10k road race came 55th time (43.50.58)

Tue 27th} 220 press-ups 180 on press-up stands (40,40,30,30,30,30,20)

Wed 28th} 31 min jog

JUNE 2003

Mon 2nd} went to bodyworks gym plus 25 min's on the bag

Tue 3rd} 20 min's stomach workout

Wed 4th} 32 min jog

Sat 7th} 3-mile jog time (20.18.54) a p.b.

Mon 9th} went to bodyworks gym plus 31 min jog

Thu 12th} 30 min jog

Sun 15th} 42 min jog

Wed 18th} went to bodyworks gym

Thu 19th} 31 min jog

Sat 21st} Datchet Dash 10k road race time (44.04.67)

Mon 23rd} went to bodyworks gym plus 20 min's on the bag

Tue 24th} 31 min jog

Sat 28th} 30 min jog

Mon 30th} went to bodyworks gym

JULY 2003

Thu 3rd} 29 min jog

Sun 6th} Sam Run multi terrain 10k race time (43.32.10)

Wed 9th} 3-mile jog time (20.32.71)

Sun 13th} went to the running track done 6 laps

Mon 14th} went to bodyworks gym plus 15 min's on the bag

Mon 21st} went to bodyworks gym

Mon 28th} went to bodyworks gym

AUG 2003

Mon 4th} 14 min jog plus 10 min's on the bag

Mon 11th} went to bodyworks gym

Tue 12th} 205 press-ups on stands (20,40,30,30,30,20,15,20)

Sun 17th} 3-mile jog time (22.47.06)

Mon 18th} went to bodyworks gym

Thu 21st} 3-mile jog time (22.00.04}

Mon 25th} 210 press-ups on stands plus 109 pull-ups (67 with weights)

Tue 26th} 22 min jog plus 20 min's on the bag and went swimming

Fri 29th} 3-mile jog time (21.20.89)

SEP 2003

Mon 1st} went to bodyworks gym

Thu 4th} 31 min jog

Sun 7th} 33 min jog

Tue 9th} 3-mile jog time (21.30.54)

Fri 12th} 32 min jog

Wed 17th} 17 min jog

Sun 21st} 3-mile jog time (22.24.20) plus 100 press-ups on stands

Wed 24th} 29 min jog

Mon 29th} 37 min jog

OCT 2003

Thu 2nd} 39 min jog

Sun 5th} Camberley 10k road race time (43.41.46)

Mon 6th} went to bodyworks gym

Mon 13th} 15 min jog plus 25 min's on the bag

Mon 20th} went to bodyworks gym

NOV 2003

Sat1st} went to bodyworks gym

Mon 10th} went to bodyworks gym

Sun 16th} went mountain bike riding

Mon 17th} full body workout at home

Mon 24th} went to bodyworks gym

Fri 28th} 20 min's on the bag

DEC 2003

Mon 1st} went to bodyworks gym

Mon 15th} 3-mile jog time (23.16.70)

Mon 22nd} went to bodyworks gym

Tue 30th} 205 press-ups, 155 on stands (50,25,30,10,30,20,10,15,15)

2004

JAN 2004

Mon 5th} went to bodyworks gym

Sun 11th} went swimming

Mon 12th} 20 min's on the bag plus 16 min jog

Sun 18th} 120 arm curls, 100 sit-ups, 309 press-ups, 100 pull-ups and a 3-mile jog

Thu 22nd} 100 press-ups 20.50.30

Fri 23rd} 3-mile jog

Mon 26th} went to bodyworks gym

Thu 29th} 3-mile jog

FEB 2004

Mon 2nd} went to bodyworks gym

Fri 6th} 3-mile jog

Mon 9th} 33 min jog

Thu 12th} 3-mile jog

Tue 17th} 33 min jog

Tue 24th} 3-mile jog

Thu 26th} 3-mile jog

Sat 28th} 150 press-ups (50,50,50)

MARCH 2004

Mon 1st} went to bodyworks gym

Thu 4th} 27 min jog plus 10 min's on the bag

Sun 7th} 27 min jog

Mon 8th} 204 press-ups on stand's, 50 pull-ups, 110 sit-ups

Wed 10th} 3-mile jog

Sun 14th} 30 min jog plus 20 min's on the bag

Wed 17th} 3-mile jog

Mon 22nd} went to bodyworks gym

Wed 24th} 3mile jog

Mon 29th} 33 min jog

APRIL 2004

Thu 1st} 26 min jog

Sun 4th} 33 min jog

Thu 8th} 31 min jog plus 200 press-ups on stand's (40,30,40,30,20,15,15,10)

Sun 11th} 29 min jog plus 20 min's on the bag

Tue 13th} 31 min jog

Fri 16th} 31 min jog

Mon 19th} went to bodyworks gym

Thu 22nd} 32 min jog

Sun 25th} 40 min jog

Wed 28th} 39 min jog

Fri 30th} 22 min jog

MAY 2004

Mon 3rd} 31 min jog plus 20 min's on the bag

Tue 4th} went to bodyworks gym

Thu 6th} 41 min jog

Sun 9th} 31 min jog

Wed 12th} 22 min jog

Sat 15th} 301 press-ups

Mon 17th} 32 min jog

Wed 19th} 22 min jog

Sat 22nd} 33 min jog

Mon 24th} 25 min jog

Tue 25th} 20 min's on the bag

Fri 28th} 30 min jog

Sun 30th} went to bodyworks gym

Mon 31st} 30 min jog

JUNE 2004

Thu 3rd} 21 min jog

Sun 6th} 40 min jog

Tue 8th} 22 min jog

Fri 11th} 33 min jog

Sun 13th} 240 press-ups (30,40,30,30,30,40,20,20)

Mon 14th} 41 min jog

Wed 16th} 22 min jog

Sun 20th} 41 min jog

Tue 22nd} went to bodyworks gym

Wed 23rd} 39 min jog, 15min's on the bag plus 100 press-ups

Fri 25th} 28 min jog

Sun 27th} 31 min jog

Tue 29th} 32 min jog

JULY 2004

Sat 3rd} Dorney Dash 10k road race, time in (44.14.66)

Sun 4th} Sam Run 10k race, time in (43.55.11)

Mon 5th} 100 arm curls on each arm with 14kg plus 70 pull-ups

Wed 7th} 23 min jog

Mon 12th} went to bodyworks gym

Wed 14th} 31 min jog

Mon 19th} 29 min jog

Thu 22nd} 23 min jog

Su 25th} went to bodyworks gym

Mon 26th} 37 min jog

Wed 28th} 14 min jog plus 20 min's on the bag

Sat 31st} 39 min jog plus 50 arm curls on each arm

AUG 2004

Tue 3rd} 22 min jog

Thu 5th} 301 press-ups plus 100 arm curls on each arm with 14kg

Sun 8th} Midhurst 10k road race, time in (48.10.03)

Wed 11th} 21 min jog

Sat 14th} 21 min jog

Mon 16th} went to bodyworks gym plus 38 min jog

Wed 18th} 22 min jog

Sun 22nd} 21 min jog

Mon 23rd} 37min jog plus 200 press-ups

Thu 26th} 30 min jog

Sun 29th} 49 min jog

Mon 30th} 30 min jog

SEPT 2004

Wed 1st} 28 min jog

Sun 5th} Oracle-to-Oracle 10k road race, time in (45.09.28)

Mon 6th} went to bodyworks gym

Wed 8th} 20 min's on the bag

Thu 9th} 32 min jog

Fri 10th} went to bodyworks gym

Wed 15th} 18 min jog

Thu 16th} 200 press-ups

Mon 20th} 39 min jog

Thu 23rd} 22 min jog

Sun 26th} Camberley 10k road race, time in (44.55.16)

OCT 2004

Sun 3rd} went to bodyworks gym

Mon 4th} 14 min jog plus 25 min's on the bag

Sun 10th} 250 press-ups 100 pull-ups

Mon 11th} 20 min jog

Mon 18th} went to bodyworks gym

Sun 31st} went to bodyworks gym

Nov 2004

Sun 7th} 21 min jog

Wed 10th} 22 min jog plus 20 min's on the bag

Thu 11th} went to bodyworks gym

Mon 22nd} 24 min jog

Sun 28th} 26 min jog

Mon 29th} went to bodyworks gym

Dec 2004

Thu 2nd} 23 min jog

Sun 5th} 42 min jog

Tue 7th} 23 min jog

Fri 10th} 23 min jog

Sun 12th} 44 min jog plus 20 min's on the bag

Tue 14th} 250 press-ups

Wed 15th} 23 min jog

Fri 17th} 23 min jog

Sun 19th} 1hr 24 min jog

Wed 22nd} 23 min jog

Sun 26th} 57 min jog

Mon 27th} 250 press-ups, 100 pull-ups with weights, 50 leg raises with weights

Tue 28th} 24 min jog

Wed 29th} 150 arm curls with 14kg 100 sit-ups with 4.5 kg

Thu 30th} 56 min jog

2005

JAN 2005

Sun 2nd} 62 min jog

Mon 3rd} went to bodyworks gym

Wed 5th} 23 min jog

Sun 9th} 65 min jog

Tue 11th} 23 min jog

Mon 17th} 56 min jog

Wed 19th} 23 min jog

Sun 23rd} 70 min jog

Mon 24th} went to bodyworks gym

Wed 26th} 23 min jog

Fri 28th} 24 min jog

Mon 31st} 85 min jog

Feb 2005

Fri 4th} 23min jog

Sun 6th} 93 min jog

Wed 9th} 22 min jog

Sun 13th} Wokingham half marathon time in (2.03.40)

Mon 14th} 15 min's on the bag

Tue 15th} 260 press-ups (200 with press-up stands)

Thu 17th} 100 arm curls on each arm with 14kg

Mon 21st} went to bodyworks gym

MARCH 2005

Thu 3rd} went to bodyworks gym

Wed 9th} 23 min jog

Thu 17th} went to bodyworks gym

Mon 28th} 24 min jog

April 2005

Fri 1st} 23 min jog

Sat 2nd} 255 press-ups (195 with stands)

Mon 4th} 23 min jog

Fri 8th} 22 min jog

Tue 12th} 24 min jog

Sun 17th} 23 min jog plus 265 press-ups (155 with stands)

Tue 19th} went to bodyworks gym

Fri 22nd} 35 min jog

Mon 25th} 34 min jog

Thu 28th} 23 min jog

MAY 2005

Sun 1st} 40 min jog

Tue 3rd} went to bodyworks gym

Wed 4th} 22 min jog

Sun 8th} 40 min jog

Wed 11th} 24 min jog

Sun 15th} 42 min jog plus 25 min's on the bag

Tue 17th} 22 min jog

Thu 19th} 40 min jog

Sun 22nd} Staines/Spelthorn 10k road race time in (44.40.09)

Tue 24th} 250 press-ups (200 with stands) plus 70 curls on each arm with 14kg

Mon 30th} 24 min jog

Tue 31st} went to bodyworks gym

JUNE 2005

Thu 2nd} 24 min jog

Mon 6th} 39 min jog

Thu 9th} 23min jog

Mon 13th} 39 min jog

Wed 15th} 23 min jog

Sun 19th} 265 press-ups (215 with stands)

Mon 20th} 50 min jog

Thu 23rd} 23min jog

Mon 27th} 31 min jog plus 20 min's on the bag

JULY 2005

Sun 3rd} 10k Sam Run time in (45.30.75)

Tue 5th} went to bodyworks gym

Wed 6th} 50 leg raises on the pull-up bar with leg weights

Thu 7th} 50 pull ups (40 with leg weights) plus a 23 min jog

Sun 10th} 38 min jog

Wed 13th} 23 min jog

Fri 15th} 23 min jog

Sat 16th} 260 press-ups (210 with stands)

Tue 19th} 33 min jog

Thu 21st} 22 min jog

Sun 24th} 39 min jog

Wed 27th} 23 min jog

Sun 31st} 42 min jog

AUG 2005

Wed 3rd} 38 min jog

Mon 8th} 60 min jog

Thu11th} 156 arm curls on each arm with 14kg

Sun 14th} Midhurst 10k road race time in (46.21.02)

Tue 16th} went to bodyworks gym

Thu 18th} 23 min jog

Sun 21st} 60 min jog

Wed 24th} 23 min jog

Fri 26th} 260 press-ups (190 with stands)

Sun 28th} 60 min jog

Tue 30th} 21 min jog plus 15 min's on the bag

SEP 2005

Sun 4th} 10 min jog

Tue 6th} went to bodyworks gym

Sun 18th} 34 min jog

Mon 19th} 100 arm curls with 14kg

Wed 21st} 24 min jog

Sun 25th} 60 min jog

Wed 28th} 22 min jog

Fri 30th} 260 press-ups (210 with stands)

OCT 2005

Sun 2nd} Camberley 10k road race time in (44.37.48)

Tue 4th} 23 min jog

Sat 8th} 60 min jog

Tue 11th} 38 min jog

Fri 14th} 159 pull-ups (87 with weights), 100 arm curls with 14kg, 100 sit-ups

Sun 16th} Legoland Prince's Trust 10k time in (45.53.93)

Thu 20th} 22 min jog

Sun 30th} went to bodyworks gym

NOV 2005

Tue 8th} 23 min jog

Mon 14th} 250 press-ups (200 with stands 50,40,30,30,15,25,20,20,20,)

Mon 21st} 22 min jog plus 20 min's on the bag

Mon 28th} went to bodyworks gym

DEC 2005

Fri 2nd} 22 min jog

Thu 8th} 23 min jog

Tue 20th} 23 min jog

Fri 23rd} 389 press-ups (289 with stands)

Fri 30th} went to bodyworks gym

2006

JAN 2006

Mon 2nd} 21 min jog plus 15 min's on the bag

Thu 12th} 23 min jog

Wed 25th} 23min jog

Mon 30th} 23 min jog

Tue 31st} 359 press-ups (247 with stands)

FEB 2006

Fri 3rd} 23 min jog

Thu 9th} 23 min jog

Mon 13th} 23 min jog

Wed 15th} went to bodyworks gym

Sat 18th} 34 min jog

Tue 21st} 23 min jog

Sat 25th} 38 min jog

Tue 28th} 23 min jog

MARCH 2006

Fri 3rd} 32 min jog

Mon 6th} 32 min jog

Thu 9th} 38 min jog

Sun 12th} 42 min jog

Mon 13th} 15 min's on the bag

Thu 16th} 37 min jog

Sun 19th} 54 min jog

Mon 20th} 50 min jog

Fri 24th} 115 leg raises with weights plus 100 pull-ups (53 with ankle weights)

Sun 26th} Frimley Park Hospital 10k time in (44.54.95)

Wed 29th} 22 min jog

APRIL 2006

Mon 3rd} 38 min jog plus 5-mile bike ride

Thu 6th} 38 min jog

Fri 7th} 257 press-ups (117 with stands)

Sat 8th} went to bodyworks gym

Mon 10th} 38 min jog

Fri 14th} 38 min jog

Mon 17th} 40 min jog plus 15 min's on the bag

Thu 20th} 21 min jog

Sun 23rd} 40 min jog

Tue 25th} 22 min jog

Sun 30th} 38 min jog

MAY 2006

Wed 3rd} 36 min jog

Fri 5th} 21 min jog

Sun 7th} 145 arm curls on each arm with 12kg plus 283 press-ups (133 with stands)

Tue 9th} 35 min jog

Sat 13th} 42 min jog

Mon 15th} 53 min jog

Thu 18th} 21 min jog

Sun 21st} Staines 10k road race time in (43.04.47)

Thu 25th} 22 min jog

Fri 26th} 120 leg raises on pull up bar 80 with ankle weights

Sun 28th} went to bodyworks gym

Tue 30th} went swimming

JUNE 2006

Sun 4th} 37 min jog

Fri 9th} 30 min's on the bag

Sun 11th} went to bodyworks gym

Mon 19th} 22 min jog

Fri 23rd} 38 min jog

Mon 26th} 54 min jog

JULY 2006

Sun 2nd} 10k Sam run race 33 degrees time in (48.39.60)

Fri 7th} 302 press-ups (102 with stands) plus sit-ups and leg raises

Sun 16th} went for mountain bike ride

Tue 18th} 110 arm curls on each arm with 14kg plus 100 sit-ups

Sun 23rd} went to bodyworks gym

AUG 2006

Mon 7th} 14 min jog

Thu 10th} 20 min's on the bag

Fri 11th} 14 min jog

Mon 14th} 1hr 45min's mountain bike ride (really tough) at the look-out with Martin

Wed 16th} 24 min jog

Sat 19th} 24 min jog

Sun 20th} went to bodyworks gym

Wed 23rd} 39 min jog

Fri 25th} 22 min jog

Tue 29th} 45 min jog

Thu 31st} 23 min jog

SEP 2006

Sun 3rd} 020 10k road race along the river time in (48.24.97)

Sun 10th} 255 press-ups (50 with stands) 105 sit-ups plus went swimming

Wed 20th} 20 min jog

Sun 24th} went to bodyworks gym

OCT 2006

Sun 1st} 3k fun run with Rebecca and Danielle

Sun 8th} went to bodyworks gym

Sun 22nd} 23 min jog

Mon 30th} 302 press-ups (72 with stands) plus100 sit-ups

NOV 2006

Wed 1st} 100 sit-ups

Sun 5th} went to bodyworks gym

Mon 19th} 23 min jog plus 100 arm curls on each arm with 14kg plus boxercise

Mon 27th} went to bodyworks gym

DEC 2006

Sat 16th} 305 press-ups (100 with stands) plus 100 sit-ups

Sun 24th} went to bodyworks gym

2007

JAN 2007

Mon 1st} 24 min jog

Mon 15th} 23 min jog

Fri 19th} 306 press-ups 100 sit-ups 52 pull-ups

Sun 21st} went to bodyworks gym plus 24 min jog

Thu 25th} 24 min jog

Tue 30th} 22 min jog plus 20 min's on the bag

FEB 2007

Sun 11th} 42 min jog

Tue 13th} 100 press-ups

Wed 14th} 23 min jog

Sun 18th} 41 min jog

Tue 20th} 24 min jog

Fri 23rd} 23 min jog

Sun 25th} 40 min jog

Wed 28th} 23 min jog

MAR 2007

Sun 4th} 40 min jog

Tue 6th} 39 min jog

Thu 8th} 23 min jog

Sun 11th} 45 min jog

Tue 13th} 38 min jog

Sun 18th} Frimley Park 10k road race time in (47.26.39)

Mon 19th} 375 press-ups 110 sit-ups plus 100 arm curls on each arm with 14kg

Fri 23rd} 22 min jog

Mon 26th} 39 min jog

Wed 28th} 22 min jog

ARIL 2007

Sun 1st} 44 min jog

Mon 2nd} 20 min's on the bag

Wed 4th} 38 min jog

Sat 7th} 39 min jog 200 arm curls 100 press-ups 100 sit-ups

Tue 10th} went to bodyworks gym

Wed 11th} 22 min jog

Fri 13th} 38 min jog

Sat 14th} went swimming

Mon 16th} 43 min jog

Wed 18th} 22 min jog

Mon 23rd} 54 min jog

Tue 24th} 340 press-ups

Thu 26TH} 22 min jog

Sun 29th} 42 min jog

Mon 30th} 25 min's on the bag

MAY 2007

Thu 3rd} 38 min jog

Sun 6th} 42 min jog

Tue 8th} went to bodyworks gym

Thu 10th} 36 min jog

Sun 13th} 22 min jog

Sun 20th} Staines 10k road race time in (43.41.95)

Tue 22nd} 300 press-ups 110 pull-ups

Wed 23rd} 22 min jog

Mon 28th} 38 min jog

Tue 29th} 302 press-ups

Wed 30th} 32 min jog

JUNE 2007

Mon 4th} 37 min jog

Wed 6th} 22 min jog

Sun 10th} 43 min jog

Wed 13th} 36 min jog

Fri 15th} 22 min jog

Mon 18th} 37 min jog

Wed 20th} 21 min jog

Sun 24th} 44 min jog plus 20 min's on the bag

Mon 25th} 37 min jog

Thu 28th} 300 press-ups plus100 arm curls with 16kg plus 100 leg raises

JULY 2007

Sun 1st} Sam Run 10k race time in (45.09.01)

Sun 8th} 37 min jog

Wed 11th} 37 min jog

Fri 13th} 22 min jog

Mon 16th} went to bodyworks gym

Wed 18th} 37 min jog

Sun 22nd} 37 min jog

Wed 25th} 37 min jog

Thu 26th} 310 press-ups 55 with stands plus 120 sit-ups

Sun 29th} 36 min jog

Mon 30th} 32 min jog

AUG 2007

Thu 2nd} 21 min jog

Mon 6th} 38 min jog

Tue 7th} went to bodyworks gym

Thu 9th} 40 min jog plus 20 min's on the bag

Sat 11th} 37 min jog

Mon 13th} speed session; fast 300-metre jogs

Wed 15th} 42 min jog

Sat 18th} 42 min jog plus 100 arm curls on each arm with 14kg

Mon 20th} 315 press-ups (40,30,30,20,20,40,30,20,30,25,30)

Tue 21st} speed session; fast 300-metre jogs

Mon 27th} 41 min jog

Tue 28th} 21 min jog

SEPT 2007

Sun 2nd} Oracle 2 Oracle 10k road race time in (45.19.24)

Fri 7th} 205 press-ups 150 pull-ups 210 sit-ups

Mon 10th} 21 min jog

Thu 13th} 22 min jog

Sun 16th} 36 min jog

Wed 19th} 21 min jog

Sun 23rd} 41 min jog

Mon 24th} 350 press-ups 204 sit-ups

Wed 26th} 100 arm curls on each arm with 14kg plus 200 sit-ups

Thu 27th} 37 min jog

Sun 30th} 41 min jog

OCT 2007

Tue 21 min jog

Sun 7th} Camberley 10k road race time in (43.51.86)

Fri 12th} 315 press-ups 175 with stands all in 1 hour

Sun 14th} 20 min jog plus 15 min's on the bag

Tue23rd} 21 min jog plus 421 press-ups in 1 hour (381 on press-up stands)

Mon 29th} 37 min jog

Tue 30th} 100 leg raises plus 100 press-ups

NOV 2007

Mon 5th} went to bodyworks gym

Mon 19th} 23 min jog

Tue 20th} 500 press-ups (430 with stands)

Mon 26th} 22 min jog

Fri 30th} 20 min's on the bag

DEC 2007

Sun 9th} 23 min jog

Tue 11th} 453 press-ups (313 with stands) plus 100 pull-ups

Fri 21st} 150 arm curls on each arm with (14kg)

Mon 24th} 22 min jog

Sun 30th} went to body works gym

2008

JAN 2008

Mon 14th} 23 min jog

Mon 21st} 21 min jog plus 20 min's on the bag

Fri 25th} 23 min jog

Mon 28th} 23 min jog

FEB 2008

Fri 1st} 22 min jog

Mon 4th} 23 min jog plus 120 arm curls on each arm with 14kg plus 100 triceps

Fri 8th} 23 min jog plus 50 press-ups

Mon 11th} 22 min jog plus 200 sit-ups

Fri 15th} 22 min jog plus 50 press-ups

Thu 19th} 23 min jog

Wed 20th} 420 press-ups (357 with stands)

Thu 21st} 20 straight arm pull-ups in one go

Fri 22nd} 100 arm curls on each arm with 14kg plus 100 tricep extensions

Sat 23rd} 38 min jog

Wed 27th} 21 min jog

MAR 2008

Sun 2nd} 39 min jog

Wed 5th} 22 min jog

Sun 9th} 39 min jog plus 20 min's on the bag

Wed 12th} 22 min jog

Fri 14th} 20 min jog

Tue 18th} 359 press-ups (219 with stands)

Wed 19th} 22 min jog

Sat 22nd} 61 min jog

Sun 23rd} 120 pull-ups in 10's plus 150 sit-ups

Tue 25th} 20 min jog

Sun 30th} 44 min jog

APRIL 2008

Wed 2nd} 359 press-ups (189 with stands) 150 arm curls plus 220 sit-ups

Wed 9th} 19 min jog

Thu 10th} 150 pull-ups in 10's plus 200 sit-ups

Sat 12th} 37 min jog

Tue 15th} 22 min jog

Sun 20th} Frimley Park Hospital 10k road race time (46.40.09)

Tue 22nd} 370 press-ups (220 with stands) plus 170 arm curls with 14kg

Wed 23rd} 22 min jog

Sun 27th} 22 min jog

Tue 29th} 100 pull-ups in 10's plus 100 arm curls with 14kg

MAY 2008

Thu 1st} 22 min jog

Sun 4th} 38 min jog

Wed 7th} 45 min jog

Fri 9th} 22 min jog plus 100 arm curls on each arm with 14kg

Sat 10th} 20 min's on the bag

Mon 12th} 43 min jog plus 130 pull-ups

Fri 16th} 424 press-ups 100 arm curls 200 tricep extensions 200 sit-ups

Sun 18th} Stains 10k road race time (45.42.55)

Sun 25th} 23 min jog

Tue 27th} went to bodyworks gym

Thu 29th} 20 min jog plus went swimming

JUNE 2008

Mon 2nd} 23 min jog

Tue 3rd} went to bodyworks gym

Thu 5th} 44 min jog

Sun 8th} 38 min jog

Tue 10th} 250 ab-roller crunches plus 102 pull-ups

Wed 11th} 22 min jog

Sun 15th} 41 min jog plus 20 min's on the bag

Tue 17th} 22 min jog

Mon 23rd} 38 min jog

Wed 25th} 335 press-ups (125 with stands) plus 124 pull-ups and 270 sit-ups

Fri 27th} 17 min jog

Sun 29th} Sam Run 10k road race time (46.57.51)

JULY 2008

Mon 7th} 23 min jog

Thu 10th} 118 pull-ups 25,10,10,8,15,10,10,10,10,10

Fri 11th} 50 sit-ups plus 20 leg raises

Sun 13th} 22 min jog

Tue 15th} 340 press-ups (100 with stands)

Thu 17th} 22 min jog

Mon 21st} 22 min jog

Fri 25th} 54 pull-ups 120 arm curls with 14kg plus 200 tricep extensions

Mon 28th} 22 min jog

Wed 30th} 20 min's on the bag

AUG 2008

Sun 3rd} 22 min jog

Fri 8th} 345 press-ups (135 with stands) 106 pull-ups plus 230 sit-ups

Sun 17th} 24 min jog

Thu 21st} 130 arm curls (60 with 14kg, 70 with 18kg) plus 190 tricep extensions

Fri 22nd} 22 min jog

Tue 26th} 21 min jog

Sat 30th} 320 press-ups (95 with stands) plus 124 pull-ups

Sun 31st} 23 min jog plus 15 min's on the bag

SEP 2008

Fri 5th} 24 min jog

Fri 12th} 22 min jog 306 press-ups plus 118 pull-ups

Mon 15th} 22 min jog

Fri 19th} 36 min jog

Sun 21st} 15 min's on the bag

Mon 22nd} 38 min jog

Thu 25th} 40 min's on mountain bike

Sun 28th} 43 min jog plus swimming

Mon 29th} 70 arm curls on each arm with 18kg plus 160 tricep extensions

Tue 30th} 200 sit-ups with ab-roller plus 20 leg raises

OCT 2008

Wed 1st} 100 pull-ups (15,15,15,10,10,10,10,15)

Thu 2nd} went mountain bike riding

Sun 5th} Camberley 10k road race time (47.08.83)

Fri 10th} 350 press-ups (95 with stands)

Tue 14th} 23 min jog

Sun 19th} 20 min's on the bag

Mon 20th} 20 min jog

NOV 2008

Mon 3rd} 335 press-ups

Wed 5th} 24 min jog plus 114 pull-ups

Mon 10th} went to bodyworks gym

Thu 13th} 23 min jog plus 230 press-ups

Fri 14th} 25 min's on the bag

Thu 20th} 300 sit-ups with ab-roller

Tue 25th} 23 min jog

DEC 2008

Tue 2nd} 311 press-ups (106 with stands) plus 150 pull-ups

Sun 7th} 23 min jog

Tue 16th} 305 press-ups 155 pull-ups plus 120 triceps extensions with 14kg

Fri 26th} 23 min jog

Sun 28th} arm curls 50 with 14kg, 61 with 18kg plus 150 triceps extensions

Tue 30th} 23 min jog